BUYING YOUR HOME

Many young people aspire to own their own home but face a myriad of challenges such as high property prices, the need to raise a large deposit, and difficulties of getting a mortgage.

The process of buying a property is also stressful, fraught with complexity and uncertainty, and a mistake can prove very costly. This book therefore provides a much-needed step-by-step guide to help those seeking to buy a property for the first-time.

Packed with helpful and practical tips, Buying Your Home gives a complete overview of the house-buying process, including finance, legal and property aspects. The authors discuss a wide range of topics, including:

- creating the right mindset
- the pros and cons of home ownership
- how to choose a suitable property
- how to save for a deposit
- how to negotiate for a better price
- how to get a mortgage
- the steps in the house-buying process
- how to ensure that mortgage payments can always be met

The book is written by experienced property buyers who have bought multiple properties, who have worked as a mortgage adviser and financial planner and who understand personal finance. It will be essential reading for undergraduate students in the field of accounting and finance and will also appeal to the general public, particularly those seeking to buy a property for the first-time. After reading the book, readers will be able to map out a plan to buy their first property with greater confidence and make a better and more informed decision that will bring financial rewards.

Lien Bich Luu is a Chartered Financial Planner and Associate Professor in Finance at Coventry University, UK.

Ai-Quang Tonthat is a Senior Lecturer in Banking and Finance at the University of Northampton, UK.

BUYING YOUR HOME

A PRACTICAL GUIDE FOR FIRST-TIME BUYERS

LIEN BICH LUU AND AI-QUANG TONTHAT

Routledge
Taylor & Francis Group

LONDON AND NEW YORK

First published 2022
by Routledge
2 Park Square, Milton Park, Abingdon, Oxon OX14 4RN

and by Routledge
605 Third Avenue, New York, NY 10158

Routledge is an imprint of the Taylor & Francis Group, an informa business

British Library Cataloguing-in-Publication Data
A catalogue record for this book is available from the British Library

Library of Congress Cataloging-in-Publication Data
Names: Luu, Liên, 1967– author. | Tonthat, Ai-Quang, author.
Title: Buying your home : a practical guide for first-time buyers /
    Lien Bich Luu and Ai-Quang Tonthat.
Description: Abingdon, Oxon ; New York, NY : Routledge, 2022. |
    Includes bibliographical references and index.
Identifiers: LCCN 2021014079 (print) | LCCN 2021014080 (ebook)
Subjects: LCSH: House buying. | Home ownership.
Classification: LCC HD1390.5 .L88 2022 (print) |
    LCC HD1390.5 (ebook) | DDC 643/.12—dc23
LC record available at https://lccn.loc.gov/2021014079
LC ebook record available at https://lccn.loc.gov/2021014080

ISBN: 978-0-367-89597-6 (hbk)
ISBN: 978-0-367-89596-9 (pbk)
ISBN: 978-1-003-02003-5 (ebk)

Typeset in Galliard
by Apex CoVantage, LLC

To our children
Tien, Chau, Han, Nam, and Long

CONTENTS

FIGURES

TABLES

ABOUT THE AUTHORS

Lien Bich Luu is Associate Professor in Finance at Coventry University, where she teaches personal finance, retirement planning and financial planning. Lien is a Chartered Financial Planner, a fellow of the Chartered Institute of Insurance, a CFP professional and a Registered Life Planner with the Kinder Institute.

She has a PhD degree in History and taught history for ten years at university, before changing her career to become a financial planner and mortgage adviser.

Ai-Quang Tonthat is Senior Lecturer in Banking and Finance at the University of Northampton. After finishing his MBA at the Judge Business School Cambridge University, Ai-Quang worked in investment banking and fast-moving consumer goods industry before setting up his management consulting and insurance business. He now enjoys lecturing in banking and finance at the University of Northampton.

Lien and Ai-Quang bought their first property 25 years ago and became property investors six years later. They have also helped many of their friends and clients achieve their property dreams.

PREFACE

As our own children are completing their university degrees and beginning to think of how to establish their lives as independent and responsible adults, we thought of a way to pass to them our knowledge and life experience in building financial security and buying property.

The young generation is facing great challenges. Among many practical challenges of living an independent life, buying your own home is probably the most formidable that young people are facing. This book is therefore serving as a practical handbook to help the first-time buyers to overcome those challenges. The knowledge contained in this book comes from many years of our life and professional experience in the property market in the UK, as first-time buyers, as property investors and financial advisers, and then for the last decade, as university lecturers in finance, banking and investment.

In the mid-1990s, like many young professional couples of our generation seeking to establish our independence, we were renting and were often having to move from one property to another, and as a result, experiencing a high level of stress and uncertainty. In the space of five years, we had lived in several rented properties, but never had a pleasant experience. At a house shared with a landlord, we discovered that he often stood by the bathroom door to hear how much water we used, and he refused to remove the plastic cover of the new mattress so that he could return it if we moved out. Unable to bear the high degree of control and the lack of independence, we moved out after three weeks.

In desperation, we phoned an estate agent and agreed to pay the rent deposit for a studio flat that we had not even been able to view. The flat was in a block of a few hundred flats and above a busy underground station. We had to endure constant noise from approaching underground trains and sleep on a broken pulled-out sofa bed. When we asked for a replacement, the landlord sent us a single z-bed (folding bed) and so we decided to stick to the broken one. We didn't really know how we had managed to survive in the studio flat for a year!

On the day we moved out, we left the studio flat in a spotless condition, but the estate agent did not have time to come and inspect the flat. They reassured us that the deposit would be returned. However, when we chased the deposit, we were told that as the cooker was not clean, the landlord had decided to keep our one month's deposit (£495 – this amount was a lot as it was equivalent to a two weeks' salary for one of us). This experience strengthened our resolve to buy and we vowed never to rent again.

Despite our determination to buy our home, we received a lot of conflicting advice from friends and families. While most offered encouragement, a few gave scary warnings of the burden of having a debt for life, falling property prices and inability to pay mortgage payments due to increasing interest rates. Yet, no one warned us of the complicated process of buying the house. We ignored a friend's advice to use a mortgage adviser because we wanted to save money and thought that we could find a good mortgage deal ourselves as we had good salaries so any bank would lend to us. We needed a solicitor to help with the purchase and, without much research, we turned to the father of a good university friend.

Whenever we saw a property we liked, we instructed the solicitor to begin the process. Then we changed our minds, withdrew the offer and incurred substantial costs. We once agreed to buy a house and spent £1,500 on a full structural survey as well as legal fees. We then discovered that there was a heavy freight railway right behind the garden about which neither the estate agent nor the owner had told us and that there were plans to increase the use of the railway during the night. Worried about the noise, we decided to withdraw our offer.

After a few offers and cancellations, we finally settled on a semi-detached house owned by a 93-year-old gentleman. Because of the condition of the property, the surveyor valued the house at £5,000 less than the price we had agreed. This affected our mortgage because the bank now lent us less money. We asked for a small reduction in price, and the owner stubbornly refused. However, his health was deteriorating and after a few weeks, he reluctantly agreed.

We exchanged the contract and paid the deposit, and the owner moved into a nursing home. Two days later, the estate agent rang to let us know that the owner had died shortly after he moved out. His death meant our house purchase had to be postponed until his probate was sorted out. In the meantime, we had already given notice to the landlord of the studio flat. We asked the legal experts we knew how long the probate would take and the answer was the same: it could be anything from six months to a year if we were lucky.

We pleaded and begged our solicitor to do something so that we could move in because we had used all our money for the house deposit and did not have money to pay for rent. After a few weeks of endless phone calls and emails to our solicitor, we were granted permission to move in, despite not being able to complete the sale. In other words, we moved in without being the legal owner of the house.

We had no bed and had to sleep on a mattress borrowed from a friend. Then we discovered that the electricity in the house had been last inspected in the 1960s, so it needed a complete rewiring. The boiler broke down because it was installed in 1960s.

And then came the bill from our solicitor. It was nearly £6,000 (the average cost was £500). To our shock and dismay, for every phone call we made to our solicitor he had clocked it and charged us £5 per minute; and for every email he sent out to us he charged £20, and every email he sent to the seller's solicitor he charged £35. While we were struggling to pay the solicitor's fees and the costs of installing a new boiler and buying some basic furniture, one of us was about to be made redundant as the result of the Asian financial crisis.

Moreover, the mortgage deal we got from a building society was 7.49 per cent fixed for five years. Within six months of starting the mortgage, interest rates dropped drastically but we could not benefit as we had a fixed rate. After a few years, we needed some money and changing our mortgage to another bank meant we had to pay a hefty penalty charge of more than £7,000. But despite all that, we have managed to survive.

Our experience of buying a house is not the normal experience that most first-time buyers go through, but it shows that the process is complicated, full of uncertainties and many things can go wrong. We also paid a heavy price for a lack of experience, knowledge and understanding. We therefore wrote this book to help you understand the process so that you can avoid the costly mistakes we made.

If you wish to buy and own a property for the first-time, we hope that this book will give you clear guidance, many useful tips and a great deal of support.

Good luck with your purchase and enjoy your journey to homeownership.

ACKNOWLEDGEMENTS

We have received a lot of help and support with the publication of this book. We are extremely grateful to our editor, Kristina Abbotts, whose help, enthusiasm, encouragement and support ensured that the proposal was translated into a book. We are also lucky to have received the support of the editorial board and the anonymous reviewers. We also would like to thank the editorial assistant, Christiana Mandizha, and the production team for their help and support.

This book has greatly benefited from the feedback from some of the undergraduate students at Bristol and Coventry University. We would like to thank Tien Tonnu, Zack Briggs, Hannah Nolan and Karamdeep Rai for their invaluable comments on the draft book chapters. We hope you will be pleased with the final version. Finally, we would like to thank Alan Marchant for his helpful comments and proof-reading.

Chapter One
Why should you buy?

Home ownership has become a national obsession in the UK, and an overwhelming majority of young people want to buy their own home. A Santander First-Time Buyer Study in 2019 shows that over 91 per cent of young people interviewed aspire to climb the property ladder (Santander, 2019). Home ownership thus has become an important priority for young people, and this is fostered by a wide range of social, economic and psychological factors.

Motivations for home ownership

There are many compelling reasons why many of us desire to own our own home. We all need somewhere to live, and housing is an essential need. Yet, there are not enough homes in the UK to meet demand and the shortage is estimated at one million homes (Gompertz, 2020). The demand for housing is growing due to rising population, increasing life expectancy, high rates of divorce and the number of people living by themselves. However, the supply is restricted, due to the UK being an island country, and the rate of new houses being built has historically always been lagging behind the demand.

A second reason relates to our desire for decent and quality housing. When renting, we might pay high rents, but rental properties are sometimes poorly maintained because landlords may not carry out our requests for repairs, and we may have restrictions on how we use the property (e.g. no pets). In addition, the quality of housing might be poor, the furniture unsuitable and living condition cramped. In fact, it is found that those who own their homes not only spend less money on housing but also enjoy a better lifestyle because they have more space (an extra 4 m² each over those who rent) (Savage, 2018).

There are also long-term financial benefits associated with owning a property. Sometimes, the monthly outlay to buy a home is little different from the amount paid in rent, but the big difference lies in your future economic security. Renting is often described as 'dead money', or 'money down the drain', because you are not building any of your own asset but enriching someone else's pockets. Buying, on the other hand, enables you to acquire an asset and forces you to save to pay this off. Once the debt has been paid, you can live for free, whereas if you rent, you will continue to pay rent in retirement and until the end of your life. The decision to rent or buy thus can affect your quality of life and financial security in the long term.

However, a more compelling factor to own concerns our desire for stability. Rental contracts do not necessarily give us the right to stay in the same house as long as we would like. We all know that private renting can be precarious as we can be asked to move out, even when we do not wish to. No-fault evictions, where private landlords evict tenants at short notice without a good reason, create a lot of uncertainty, stress and anxiety. Insecurity about housing hurts our well-being and pockets, and constant moving makes us poorer because it often involves paying fees and removal costs, and time packing, unpacking and cleaning.

Owning your home, on the other hand, generally means you can stay in the same place for as long as you choose, which avoids disruptions to your work, social life and family ties. Living in the same area for a long time allows you to build up a greater sense of belonging and to form better support networks – known as *social capital*. A more stable life saves you from stress, helps you avoid moving costs and increases your well-being (Luu, Lowe et al., 2017, Chapter 8).

Owning a place we call home also gives us some healthy psychological benefits. A home after all represents more than just a place to live. A home is a special place in our hearts because it is the hub of our family life and a place of sanctuary where we retreat for relaxation and safety. Owning a home is therefore important because not only does this symbolise our independence and adulthood but it also gives us a sense of pride and achievement.

The sense of independence when owning a home is important because it gives us a strong sense of control and freedom. Home ownership gives us the power to make physical changes to the house and garden and 'make it ours'; therefore, we have choice and an individual identity. No longer do we feel insecure, not knowing where we will be living and settled. Unless we fail to pay our mortgage payments, no one is going to force us to move out of our home.

The psychological and emotional benefits of owning a home are valued more than financial benefits. When interviewed by Santander Bank in 2019, more than 56 per cent of respondents stated that the most important reason to buy was due to the desire to have a sense of security, while economic benefits such as buying is a means of future wealth preservation (36 per cent), owning is cheaper than renting (36 per cent) and property is a smart investment (34 per cent) assume less importance (Santander, 2019).

Seen in this context, it is little wonder that getting on the housing ladder has become an important life goal for young people. Indeed, the Santander First-Time Buyer Study shows that home ownership is the top life goal for 51 per cent of respondents, followed by financial stability (40 per cent), travelling (29 per cent), getting fit (27 per cent), having children/family (27 per cent), reaching career goals (23 per cent), getting married (19 per cent) and being secure in retirement (16 per cent) (Santander, 2019). Unlike the old days when career, children and marriage came first, it is home ownership now that preoccupies the minds of young people.

Pros and cons of home ownership

Home ownership provides many benefits but there are also challenges.

The first recognized benefit is that homeownership can lead to wealth creation, which, in turn, can result in enhanced life satisfaction, better physical health and higher psychological well-being.

The second benefit is that homeownership tends to bring greater residential stability, which, in turn, is believed to produce better school performance among children and higher levels of civic engagement and social capital among adults. Traditionally, homeowners have remained in their homes considerably longer than renters. Evidence from the English Housing Survey supports this, and its 2018–19 report found that owner occupiers had lived at their current address for an average of 18 years, social renters 11.6 years and private renters 4.4 years. Among the private renters, 10 per cent had lived in the sector for less than one year (English Housing Survey, 2018–19). Private renters, thus, experience a highest level of residential instability.

The third benefit is that homeowners enjoy better quality housing. Compared to renters, homeowners tend to live in a house, often with gardens, and this type of housing provides a more stimulating environment for their children because they have somewhere to play and run around. As they own their property, there is a greater incentive in carrying out improvements and repairs to enhance their enjoyment and the value of their home. Thus, homeowners enjoy more control over their homes and a heightened sense of personal accomplishment and social status. This, in turn, leads to greater life satisfaction and psychological well-being.

Homeownership, however, does not always confer positive benefits. Some academics argue that homeownership can trap households, particularly those from ethnic minority and lower-income backgrounds, in areas that they would rather leave. Compared to renters, homeowners face higher transaction costs and their homes may be worth less than

Table 1.1 Pros and cons of home ownership

Positive impact	Expected benefits/liabilities
Anticipation of/actual wealth creation	Improved health, enhanced life satisfaction, improved parenting
Greater residential stability/ security	Higher levels of high school and post-secondary completions, social capital, civic engagement
Better quality housing/home environment	Better school performance and youth behaviours, greater residential satisfaction, greater self-esteem
Better quality neighbourhood: physical and social	Better schools lead to better educational outcomes, and higher homeownership rates lead to enhanced social capital and less crime
Heightened sense of control/ social status/accomplishment	Higher levels of life satisfaction and psychological health
Negative impact	*Negative benefits*
Mobility restrictions	Homeowners have more difficulty moving to better homes and neighbourhoods
Mortgage payment stress and repossession	Some homeowners experience considerable stress and other psychological problems
Home maintenance and repair stress/impacts	Some homeowners cannot afford to maintain their homes which may lead to health problems

Source: Rohe and Lindblad, 'Re-examining the Social Benefits of Homeownership' (2013)

they owe on their mortgages (known as negative equity). However, a careful choice of property can help avoid negative equity.

Other challenges include difficulties in paying mortgage payments or carrying out repairs, and this can produce a high level of financial and psychological stress. However, planning for the future and taking out a suitable insurance policy can help address these issues.

Overall, the benefits of home ownership can outweigh the challenges, but you need to take appropriate steps to ensure that you buy in the right area and that you can always pay your mortgage.

Factors influencing home ownership

A study by Rohe and Lindblad (2013) for Harvard University argues that the tenure decision – to buy or rent – is a function of both the desire and the capacity to own. The desire to own is influenced by perceived benefits, cultural attitudes, promotion of home ownership by the government, estate agents, builders and others involved in the housing industry, and views about future house prices, as illustrated in Figure 1.1.

The authors argue that the perceived benefits are also affected by both direct and indirect experience with home ownership. This influence may be direct – individuals have a bad home ownership experience themselves – or indirect – they know someone who has had a good or bad home ownership experience.

In addition to the desire to own, home ownership is also influenced by the capacity to own. That capacity is determined by the amount of deposit required, availability of suitable property and mortgages, property prices, interest rates, affordability, and earnings levels. These factors, in turn, are affected by the state of the economy, government policies and lending practices.

Although the desire to own is high among young people, their capacity to own is now curbed by a wide range of economic and social factors. These will be discussed below.

Barriers to home ownership

Climbing the property ladder now is much more difficult than before for first-time buyers. Indeed, 70 per cent of would-be first-time buyers in the UK believe that the dream of homeownership is now impossible to achieve, and thus only 30 per cent are still hopeful. Santander Bank is more pessimistic in their forecast and believes that by 2026 only 25 per cent

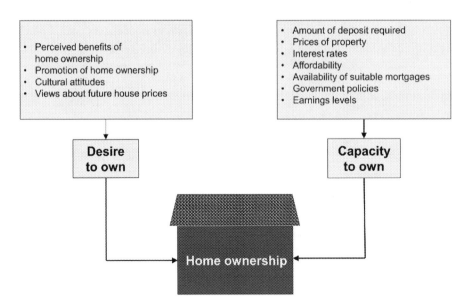

Figure 1.1 Factors affecting home ownership

Source: Adapted from Rohe and Lindblad, 'Re-examining the Social Benefits of Homeownership' (2013)

of young people between 25 and 34 years old will own their own home (Santander, 2019).

The reasons why many young people have given up hopes of owning their own home are not hard to find. To start with, house prices have risen exponentially. In 1991, an average property in the UK cost around £57,000, and by 2018, the average price has increased to more than £225,000 – a nearly fourfold increase in 27 years or nearly 15 per cent growth per annum (Land Registry, UK House Price Index, 2020).

Rapid increases in house prices make property prices unaffordable because wages have not kept up. While house prices in England have risen by 173 per cent over the past two decades, the average pay for 25- to 34-year-olds has grown by just 19 per cent over the same time period (Hampson, 2020).

Further evidence that property prices have become unaffordable can be seen in the changes to house price to earnings ratios which show how

Table 1.2 House price to earnings ratios

Year	1997	2002	2007	2010	2014	2017	2019
England	3.54	5.12	7.15	6.85	7.09	7.92	7.83
London	4	6.57	7.94	8.24	10.08	12.38	12.05

Source: Office for National Statistics, House price to workplace-based earnings ratio (2020), Office for National Statistics, Housing affordability in England and Wales (2019)

many years of salary are needed to pay for a house. In 1997, for example, the house price to earnings ratio was 3.54 for England and 4 for London. This means, on average the price of a property was equivalent to 3.5 times gross annual salary. Ten years later, by 2007, the house price to earnings had almost doubled to over 7 and nearly 8, for England and London, respectively. By 2017, while the house price-to-earnings ratio for England remained at approximately 8, it rose sharply to more than 12 for London. The good news is that prices appear to be stable, and by 2019, the ratios have not changed much.

Despite the massive increase in house price-to-earnings ratio, mortgage lending criteria have not kept pace. Before the financial crisis of 2008, a high street bank or building society typically lent between 3 and 3.5 times your gross salary. This means that if your annual salary then were £20,000, the bank would lend you between £60,000 and £70,000. Now the bank could offer up to 4 or 4.5 times your gross salary. Based on 4.5 times salary, a person on a salary of £30,000 can borrow £135,000, but this is well short of the amount needed to buy an average property in the UK.

What's more, lending criteria have become even stricter after the 2008 financial crisis. A series of banking regulations has been enforced to ensure the stability of the banking industry, and the fair treatment of retail borrowers has led to much stricter lending criteria. Banks are now required to ensure that a person can afford a mortgage loan before lending.

The rapid rate of house price increase has also presented another great challenge for young people to get on the property ladder because as the price rises, they need to put down a bigger deposit which means they need a longer time to save for it. As lenders no longer offer a 100 per cent mortgage, buyers need to put down as a deposit a minimum of 5 per cent of the value of a property. With an average house price of £247,000 in the UK and £477,000 in London in December 2019 (UK House Price Index – Office for National Statistics, 2020), borrowers would need to have a deposit of £12,350 and £23,850, respectively, assuming that their salaries are high enough to support the loan.

Research from the Halifax bank found that the average home deposit in the UK is £33,000, but the Money Charity reported that in October 2019, the average first-time buyer house deposit in fact was £48,500. With an average saving rate of 6.8 per cent of post-tax income, the Money Charity believes it would take 25 years for someone on an average salary to afford the average first-time buyer deposit (The Money Charity, 2020). In London, first-time buyers are expected to scrape together around £106,000 or 26 per cent of the average house price in the capital (Hampson, 2020). High property prices and the need for a big deposit, therefore, have made many young people lose the hope of ever getting on the property ladder.

But before you feel any despair, there are many sources of help available.

Help available to first-time buyers

Despite formidable challenges discussed above, many first-time buyers have succeeded in achieving their dream of buying their own property. In 2018, a total of 370,000 mortgages or 30,833 mortgages per month, worth £62 billion, were given to first-time buyers. In August 2019, the monthly number of first-time buyers buying their own property reached a 12-year high at 35,010 completions. This figure is comparable to the previous high in August 2007, when there were 35,070 new first-time buyer mortgages completed (Gov.UK, 2020).

First-time buyers, therefore, should not feel despair because, in truth, there is a lot of help available from the government, lenders, parents, employers and mortgage advisers.

Firstly, the government is offering a helping hand, with the Help to Buy Equity Loan Scheme and stamp duty exemption for first-time buyers, designed to help with the problem of raising the deposit and paying upfront costs. Most recently, in response to the withdrawal of high loan to value mortgages, the Government has promised to guarantee mortgages up to 95 per cent to encourage lenders to offer 95 per cent mortgages so that first-time buyers only need to put down a five per cent deposit. These will be discussed more in Chapter 7.

Secondly, lenders have introduced a host of innovative products to help first-time buyers. To tackle the challenge of raising a deposit, for example, lenders allow applicants to use family and friend's savings as security. Lending innovations will be discussed in more detail in Chapter 8.

You can also get professional help to increase your chance of getting a mortgage. There are many specialist lenders out there who offer innovative products (e.g. rent-a-room mortgage where lenders incorporate potential rental income in the affordability calculations) but their mortgages are often only available via professional advisers. Using a professional adviser can increase your chance of getting a mortgage. A recent study showed that nearly nine in ten first-time buyers (88 per cent) applying through an intermediary secured a mortgage offer (Halifax Intermediaries, 2018). In the UK, there are many mortgage advisers (estimated 16,000 brokers) who can help you get a mortgage (Barker and Barker, 2018).

Thirdly, many parents are stepping in to help their children to buy their first home. As property prices soar, parents may have seen the value of their own home increased and they can use this wealth to help their children. In 2019, Legal & General estimated that the 'Bank of Mum and Dad' lent a staggering £6.3 billion to their children to buy a property, making it effectively the ninth biggest lender in the UK (Legal and General, 2019).

Fourthly, some employers are also making interventions. In London, the shortage of affordable homes is making business leaders anxious, as many see high housing costs affecting their recruitment at junior levels. Some companies are reassessing how they can use perks to attract top talent and are considering offering help in meeting housing costs, such as loans, subsidies or mortgage deals. Some, for example, have arranged preferential mortgage rates for employees with leading banks, while others have negotiated special rental terms for its employees, including free superfast broadband, free rent for two weeks, no deposit and no registration fees (Forrest, 2018).

The following chapters of this book will help you develop strategies not only to overcome the adverse challenges but also to make the most of the favourable opportunities to climb the housing ladder.

It also offers a simple and step-by-step manual to the house-buying process. It shows you how to create the right mindset to buy and own a house. It helps you make informed decisions and gives you the tools and techniques to manage risks throughout the house-buying process. With this knowledge and insights, we hope you will approach the house-buying process with a holistic view and greater confidence, and avoid costly mistakes.

References

Barker, S., and Barker, S., 2018, 'FCA Data Sheds Light on Mortgage Broker Numbers', *Money Marketing*, 30 April 2018 [online]. Available at www.moneymarketing.co.uk/news/fca-reveals-mortgage-broker-figures/ [Accessed 12 November 2020].

English Housing Survey, Headline Report 2018–19, Assets.publishing.service.gov.uk. 2020 [online]. Available at https://assets.publishing.service.gov.uk/government/uploads/system/uploads/attachment_data/file/860076/2018-19_EHS_Headline_Report.pdf [Accessed 12 November 2020].

Forrest, A., 2018, 'Top Employers Are Helping with City Housing', *Raconteur*, 22 June 2018 [online]. Available at www.raconteur.net/business-innovation/employers-help-housing [Accessed 12 November 2020].

Gompertz, S., 2020, 'Housing Shortage: Scale of UK's Housing Gap Revealed', *BBC News*, 23 February 2020 [online]. Available at www.bbc.co.uk/news/business-51605912 [Accessed 12 November 2020].

GOV.UK, 2020, *Housing Minister Hails First-Time Buyer Numbers – Now at 12 Year High* [online]. Available at www.gov.uk/government/news/housing-minister-hails-first-time-buyer-numbers-now-at-12-year-high [Accessed 12 November 2020].

Halifax Intermediaries, 2018, 'First-Time Buyers – The New Generation', *Mortgage Solutions*, 15 May 2018 [online]. Available at www.mortgagesolutions.co.uk/hub-page/2018/05/15/first-time-buyers-new-generation [Accessed 12 November 2020].

Hampson, L., 2020, 'How to Save for a Mortgage: Expert Advice on Saving for a House Deposit', *Evening Standard*, 6 January 2020 [online]. Available at www.standard.co.uk/lifestyle/london-life/how-to-save-for-a-mortgage-house-deposit-a4044686.html [Accessed 12 November 2020].

Land Registry, 2020, *UK House Price Index* [online]. Available at https://landregistry.data.gov.uk/app/ukhpi/browse?from=1991-01-01&location=http%3A%2F%2Flandregistry.data.gov.uk%2Fid%2Fregion%2Funited-kingdom&to=2018-03-01 [Accessed 12 November 2020].

Legalandgeneralgroup.com, 2019, *Bank of Mum and Dad* [online]. Available at www.legalandgeneralgroup.com/media/17339/bank-of-mum-and-dad-2019-a4-20pp.pdf [Accessed 12 November 2020].

Luu, L., Lowe, J., Butler, J., and Byrne, T., 2017, *Essential Personal Finance: A Practical Guide for Students*. London and New York: Routledge.

The Money Charity, 2020, *Money Statistics* [online]. Available at https://themoneycharity.org.uk/media/December-2019-Money-Statistics.pdf [Accessed 12 November 2020].

Office for National Statistics, 2019, *Housing Affordability in England and Wales* [online]. Available at www.ons.gov.uk/peoplepopulationandcommunity/

housing/bulletins/housingaffordabilityinenglandandwales/2018 [Accessed 12 November 2020].

Office for National Statistics, 2020, *House Price to Workplace-based Earnings Ratio* [online]. Available at www.ons.gov.uk/peoplepopulationandcommunity/ housing/datasets/ratioofhousepricetoworkplacebasedearningslowerquartile andmedian [Accessed 12 November 2020].

Office for National Statistics, 2020, *UK House Price Index* [online]. Available at www. ons.gov.uk/economy/inflationandpriceindices/bulletins/housepriceindex/ january2020 [Accessed 12 November 2020].

Rohe, W., and Lindblad, M., 2013, *Re-examining the Social Benefits of Home-ownership after the Housing Crisis.* Available at www.jchs.harvard.edu/ sites/default/files/hbtl-04.pdf [Accessed 12 November 2020].

Santander.co.uk, 2019, *Santander First-Time Buyer Study: The Future of the Homeownership Dream*, July 2019 [online]. Available at www.santander. co.uk/assets/s3fs-public/documents/santander-first-time-buyer-study.pdf [Accessed 12 November 2020].

Savage, M., 2018, 'Millennial Housing Crisis Engulfs Britain', *The Guardian*, 28 April 2018 [online]. Available at www.theguardian.com/society/2018/ apr/28/proportion-home-owners-halves-millennials [Accessed 12 November 2020].

Chapter Two

Creating the right mindset for buying your first home

When you buy your first property, whether as an individual or as a couple, you have to make probably one of the most important decisions in your life. Not only does this decision involve a large amount of money (much more than you can earn over a few years) and a long-term commitment, but it also affects your life and happiness for the foreseeable future. Such a decision therefore cannot be made on a whim, but needs a great deal of careful consideration and planning.

To buy a house is to engage in one of the most important projects of your life. Like any other projects, it has a beginning and an end, or a start and a completion. It is a journey. The journey can take weeks to complete or it can take years, depending on your starting point. Like any other journeys you have travelled or are travelling, there are turnings, stops, ups, downs, hurdles, hazards and maybe rivers to cross and mountains to climb.

And there is also YOU. Yes, you – the buyer – are the most critical factor, among many others, that determines whether the project can be started and get done or the journey can be commenced and get completed. You can learn from many people, get help from others or take advice from many experts, and you can read many books and collect mountains of data and information, but you are going on your own journey.

If you ask those who have succeeded in buying a house as first-time buyers to share their experiences, they could tell you many *hows* and many *whys*; and their experiences could vary from very easy to very difficult, or from a piece of cake to a nightmare. But they have completed their journey nevertheless.

However, if you ask the same question to those who have failed and have given up the journey, you would hear many reasons – or excuses, too. These people will never complete their journeys. And in between, there are those who have failed but have not given it up. These are still travelling on their journeys.

What is the difference between those who fail and give it up and those who have succeeded or not yet succeeded but still have not given it up?

It's obvious that people give up because they believe they can no longer complete their task or their journey, whereas others believe they can – or at least still can. So, it is just the question of belief. Some believe that they can climb any mountain if they see it in order to complete the journey, while the others believe that they cannot climb any mountain if they come across one – figuratively speaking.

What then is belief?

The American child psychologist and developmental theorist Wendy Anne McCarty (2002) offers a very clear definition of belief:

> Our beliefs are the foundation of organization of our reality. Beliefs organize and determine what we make real. They not only shape our perception of ourselves and the world, but they continue their cascading impact by shaping and directing where we focus our attention, our motives, attitudes, thoughts, feelings, choices, decisions and our actions.

Thus, your belief that you can buy a house can determine your reality of owning a house because they can shape your thinking and worldview, and they can direct your attention, motives, attitudes, thoughts, feelings, decisions and your actions.

One of the well-known management textbooks that discuss beliefs, actions and results is *Journey to the Emerald City* written by Roger Connors and Tom Smith (2002). Although the book primarily focuses on the management of cultural changes in organisations, it provides us with some very good analysis on the relationship between beliefs, actions and results. We borrow the authors' concept of the four key components that work together to produce change which are experiences, beliefs, actions and results.

According to the authors, "experiences foster beliefs, beliefs drive actions, and actions produce results" (Connors and Smith, 2002, p. 12). This model can certainly be applied to any process which seeks to produce a desired outcome – even in a personal context such as buying your own house. Here, we shall adopt the model with some minor modifications to reflect evolving and looping process of creating the right set of beliefs for buying your first home.

While focusing on creating – or changing – your beliefs, it is important not to lose sight of the key objective which is to take actions to achieve the desired outcomes. The reason for establishing the beliefs is to create a conducive environment which can facilitate the necessary actions that lead to results. Or, as McCarty (2002) says, you are creating the foundation of organisation of your reality.

But before beliefs, you need experiences. It is necessary to understand the concept of experiences here in its very broad sense which includes your own experiences, other people's experiences and advice, or even broader to include information and data that you can collect. So, experiences here equal to knowledge. This will help us create the chart in Figure 2.1.

You are encouraged to understand that actions and results in this flow chart cover any types of actions and behaviours necessary along the process of buying a house and any types of results, however small they may be, on the way to achieve your overall objective which is to buy the house. For instance, if your objective is to raise £30,000 for the deposit (result), then you can get advice on how to save money or find a way of saving money (knowledge). This will help nurture your belief that you can raise that amount of money (belief). It is the belief that you can raise enough money to pay for the deposit that drives you to reduce your

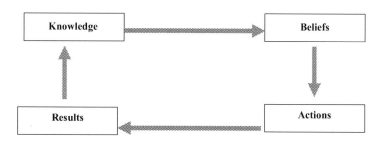

Figure 2.1 Organisation of reality

expenses, start saving, open an ISA/LISA account, find ways to earn extra income, seek some help from your parents, etc. (action).

Now, imagine you are thinking of buying a house for the first-time. Because you have never bought a house before, your belief that you can do it may not be strong enough. Therefore, you must rely on other people's experiences which often come in the form of advice, including professional advice for which you may have to pay.

Another way to strengthen your belief is to do your own research and collect information and data and do your analysis. These sources of information will foster your belief that you can buy a house. Only when you have established a belief can you then be motivated to take actions.

But beliefs themselves quite often don't necessarily lead to actions. People can believe they have the ability to do a certain thing but that doesn't mean they always take actions even just to try it out. However, as we have mentioned earlier, beliefs lay the foundation on which our reality can be perceived; it is the perception of reality that encourages us to act to achieve our goals.

Yet again, knowing the possibility does not necessarily drive actions or behaviours, but it will build our confidence. What really drives or prompts actions are key triggers. These are short-term, imminent or immediate factors, both external and internal (see more in Chapter 1).

External factors can include the Bank of England's base rate change, a government incentive programme (stamp duty exemption, tax incentive scheme, etc.), market price (being low so more affordable, or increasing and soon becoming unaffordable) or similar factors.

Internal factors are more personal such as the need to be independent, getting married, a salary increase, having sufficient savings and receiving some inheritance money. Any factor individually can be the trigger for taking actions, but any combination of them can drive actions more effectively, and in fact, the more the better.

Suppose you have got all the right advice and information (knowledge) which help you build the strong belief that you can definitely buy a house, and you have got all the necessary key triggers to prompt you to take actions, can you be certain that you will soon be the proud owner of a house?

The reason why in this book the house-buying process is likened to a journey is that it is indeed a journey. Imagine you have got all the information, and a clear direction of a certain destination, you know you can drive the car to get there, you know you must get there and you have started the engine, can you be sure that you will get there on time without any hassles?

Unfortunately, life is never straightforward. If there is time involved, there is uncertainty. If the timescale is short, there are fewer uncertainties, and if the timescale is longer, there are more uncertainties. It is uncertainties that often discourage people from completing a task or a journey. The unpredictability of events that may happen between the present and the future may not only frustrate people but also scare them off. We may call them unknown factors. Examples of unknown factors are endless and people's experiences of them can be recounted time and time again.

We could take a couple of fictitious examples: At the beginning of 2020, a young man made a New Year Resolution that he would buy a house by Christmas 2020. Little did he know that the coronavirus pandemic would hit the economy and he would be furloughed for a couple of months, and subsequently his employer would close down the company, making him redundant.

Another example: a young lady's mum and dad have promised to help her with the deposit to buy her first house from their savings. While she is searching for the house to buy and seeking mortgage advice, her father falls ill and a substantial amount from their savings has to be used for his treatment.

But between the present and the future, during the journey, there are also many certainties or many already known things – just like on a road, there may be traffic lights, sharp turns, speed bumps or even tunnels and mountain passes. These are known factors. Despite being known, the challenges they present are often underestimated. From a ten mile distance, a mountain can look much smaller than from a few hundred yards. From a few hundred yards, many potholes may not be visible.

Again, examples of these known factors are numerous. For instance, after working for two years, you have managed to save £10,000 but you need to raise an additional £20,000 in order to pay for the deposit. Raising another £20,000 would be a known challenge that you must overcome. Or another example: a man wants to buy a house and has met with a mortgage adviser and realised that his credit score is very low because he often misses his monthly credit card and car loan payments. For him to be able to borrow money from any bank he needs to repair his credit score. This known obstacle requires time and personal disciplines.

Both known and unknown factors can present a great number of challenges to first-time buyers. They can cast doubts to your experience and knowledge, shaking your beliefs and confidence. Quite often, even advice and shared experiences from other people may not help. For the journey, you need a sturdy and reliable car which you feel safe to drive and won't break down. Even if it broke down, you would have breakdown cover insurance or, at least, know how to fix it. So, you need strong mental preparedness to deal with any negative eventualities. This state of mind, or mindset, will fortify your beliefs and confidence.

Creating the mindset

The *Oxford English Dictionary (OED)* defines 'mindset' as 'a set of attitudes or fixed ideas that someone has and that are often difficult to change'. But in order to appreciate the positive impact of a right mindset, we must relate it to the fixed and growth mindset theory that is developed by the world's famous mindset guru, Caroline Dweck, Professor of Psychology at Stanford University.

In her book, *Mindset: The New Psychology of Success* (Dweck, 2007), Professor Dweck contrasts the two different mindsets. A fixed mindset is one that limits your ability to change and develop yourself. Living with this fixed mindset, you become static and confined within a certain set of characteristics and knowledge. Those with a fixed mindset have a strong fear of failure. On the contrary, a growth mindset recognises the need to change, learn and adapt to face any challenges and obstacles, facilitating personal growth. Instead of fostering fear of failure, a growth mindset facilitates hope, learning and the pursuance of success. In a growth mindset, even failure is an opportunity to learn and grow.

In another work (Blackwell et al., 2007) Prof. Dweck collaborates with her colleagues to develop a model that supports child development. We find it very useful to adopt and adapt such a model (Figure 2.2) in the context of learning to buy your first home.

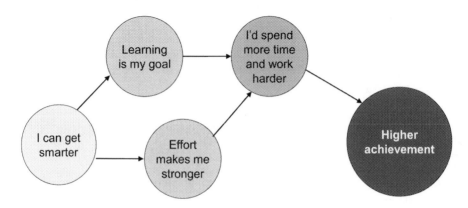

Figure 2.2 Model of learning
Source: Blackwell et al. (2007)

The model offers a practical approach to fortify your beliefs and take the correct actions to deliver the desired outcomes while continuing to develop your knowledge, build up your experience and recognise challenges ahead. You could call it the four-wheel model to build your mindset to buy your first house – as in the four wheels of the car that takes you to your destination.

For home buying, to make it easy to remember we have adapted this and translated the Blackwell, Trzesniewski and Dweck's model above into a 4-D model which stands for: Decision, Determination, Discipline and Debt.

Decision

Naturally, you will need to make a decision to buy a house when you want to buy it. But making a decision is not a simple act, especially when it involves a large amount of money and perhaps a time enduring process. What we want to share with you in this book about decision is the importance of your ability to make decisions.

Anyone can make a decision – even the decision not to make any decision. Are you someone who can always make an important decision but then often have doubt about it? Perhaps various internal or external factors cast doubt on your decision. You could have made a decision to buy your first home after saving enough for a deposit, but you look at the buying process and realise it is too complicated and full of challenges and you begin to wonder whether you should go ahead and subject yourself to the ordeal. Or, perhaps you have decided to buy a house this year but after getting advice from your family and friends, you begin to have second thoughts.

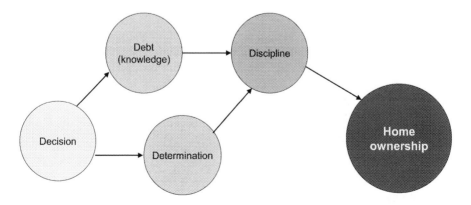

Figure 2.3 4-D model for house purchase

Whatever it is that may cause you to have doubt in your decision, be in no doubt that such thoughts are unavoidable. But doubt is like fear. It is a survival instinct. Fear protects us from doing things that may be dangerous to ourselves. Doubt helps us to be careful and cautious in what we do. But doubt is not one of our 4-Ds. Decision is. So, instead of letting doubts shake your decision, employ doubts to support it. Feel free to let doubts enter your decision-making process. Doubts are like blind spots or what you can't see approaching a bending road. You can slow down the car, watch the mirrors or use the brake. What you want to do with doubts is to call them out and confront them. Do you know that when you confront doubts, they will cease to exist? When you approach the bend, the view will be clearer and clearer. How do you know what lies ahead if you don't go forward? When you have doubt about what might happen on the road ahead, just drive there – with care and caution. If you make the decision to go there, doubt will disappear. What you see may be a clear road or some obstacles, but rest assured there is no more doubt. What is important is the decision to drive there to confront the doubt you have.

If you doubt you may never save enough money for the deposit, start saving for a few months; soon you will know whether or not you can save money. If you have doubt that the bank may not lend you the money to buy the house, go and apply for a mortgage. So, when your doubts have gone you will either have a clear road or know exactly what the obstacles are. If it's clear, keep driving forward. If it's not clear, find a way to overcome the obstacles or change your route. If you really can't save enough for the deposit, plan to save more or save for longer, or save some and borrow some from your family. If your bank turns down your mortgage application, find out why, go to a different bank or speak to a mortgage adviser. Once you have rid yourself of doubts, your decision will be stronger and so is your belief.

So, to sum up, the most important thing is to make a decision. Without a decision nothing can get done. Equally, if you make a decision and then feel unsure about it, letting doubt influence it, nothing will get done either. Your decision is invariably right if you have growth mindset which allows you to learn, develop, adapt and make changes. You might have decided to take a certain route and then later realised it is the wrong direction, but if you have a reliable car and you are patient, you will eventually get to your destination. That attitude of not giving it up calls for determination.

Determination

A decision without determination is just wishful thinking. It can be said that a decision to do something and the determination to achieve it are the two wheels on an axis. Without determination to get something done, the decision to do it is pointless. Without the decision to do something, determination to achieve it would not exist either.

When you make a decision, you expect an outcome from it. When you get into a car to drive to a destination, you have made a decision, but you only get there if you keep driving until you reach the destination. Your car may be very reliable and strong, and it has enough petrol to take you there, but getting there depends on you not stopping and turning back. So, determination is an integral part of your mindset. It's the difference between giving up and not giving up – the difference between failure and success. Unlike decisions which can be made in an instant, determination requires some time span or duration. It requires sustaining effort and involves a process. As mentioned earlier, if it involves time, then there is uncertainty. Uncertainty with determination for a journey or a process is the probability of giving it up on the way or not completing it. But, since determination is part of your mindset, you have total control of it. If you have doubts about your decision, the determination to keep going will help you clear doubts. If you meet with an obstacle that challenges your determination, then make a decision to keep going.

Within a journey or a project, determination is quite often a series of small decisions which lead to the outcome anticipated from the initial bigger decision. If you know that you cannot save £400 a month every month over a couple of years for your deposit – a question of determination – then make a decision to save £50 a week, or cut down some unnecessary expenses, or find a part-time work. If your mortgage application has been turned down by four or five banks already, then get help from a mortgage adviser, or make a decision to repair your credit score. So, determination in this context means you must keep going ahead until you reach your destination but be aware of the needs to slow down or speed up or divert to avoid obstacles – and don't give up.

On your road to acquire your first home, there will be many challenges and obstacles. They can be internal and external, personal and non-personal, emotional and financial. Therefore, once you have made the decision to buy a house you must, at the same time, condition your mind to be determined to see through the project. Knowing the challenges and obstacles and how to deal with them alone may not be enough, because of the duration factor of the project, but the ability not to give up and keep going is certainly a critical success quality.

Discipline

Now, you may be on your way to your destination and are determined to go ahead and never give up until you get there. But because you are so determined to get there soon, you drive fast and ignore the traffic lights and road warning signs. In doing so, you are at risk of not only failing to get there but also harming yourself and other people. To stay safe on the road to get to your destination, you need to follow the traffic code and abide by the law. That requires discipline.

Buying your home is very much the same – especially if it is your first-time. Imagine you have found an ideal house at an affordable price and want to exchange the contract as soon as possible. Worried that you might lose the deal, you instruct your solicitor to exchange the contract even before a local search and you ignore people's advice of a structural survey because it would take time and would be expensive. A week later, you find out the house has a major subsidence problem and the seller wants to sell it because they cannot get an insurance cover for it. What would be the outcome for you?

Examples to illustrate the need of discipline in buying and owning a house are numerous and multi-dimensional. Let's take another example. Bob believes he has saved enough money to pay for the deposit for his first home. He has also got a mortgage quote from a bank via his mort-gage adviser. While waiting to find the right house to buy, Bob misses a monthly payment on his credit card bill which leads to his credit score being downgraded. When he finds a house and agrees the price, Bob goes back to his adviser to confirm the mortgage offer. Because of his downgraded credit score, the bank withdraws the mortgage offer. Due to the lower credit score, Bob now has to reapply for a new mortgage and will have to pay a higher interest rate for his monthly mortgage pay-ment, making the mortgage unaffordable for him.

In a similar case, Alice has become a proud first-time owner of a nice city centre apartment. Her monthly mortgage payment is so high that she can't manage to save much every month. At a school reunion party, some of Alice's friends invite her to join them in a group holiday abroad. While on holiday with her friends, Alice manages to maximise her credit card limit. Fearing the high credit card interest rate, Alice uses her next three months' salaries to clear the credit balance from the holidays, causing her to miss out on her mortgage payments. She subsequently receives letters from the bank warning her of the repossession of her apartment. Can you imagine how Alice feels?

You may think those examples are rare and few and may not be relevant to you. But there are many other examples related to people losing their homes just because of a small oversight. Take an example of Joe who is also a proud owner of a nice ground floor flat. One day the household insurance renewal letter arrives, Joe sees it and plans to check for a cheaper quote online. However, because he is busy packing for his long summer holidays coming up, he thinks he can do that when he has more time during his holidays. Two weeks later while abroad, Joe only realises he has forgotten about his home insurance when he receives a phone call from his neighbour telling him that his ground floor flat has been flooded after a major storm at home. If you were in Joe's shoes, how would you feel?

The examples given earlier have shown that being a homeowner comes with many responsibilities which stretch far beyond the home purchase process; hence, being disciplined is an absolute must. However, there are two great secrets about being disciplined that you may not know. Firstly, it is part of the mindset, so you have an absolute control on it; and secondly, being disciplined or following certain disciplines can become a habit. Once it becomes a habit, it can become second nature to you. Very much similar to the disciplines to follow the highway code, at the beginning all the road signs may seem daunting because you need to pay attention and know what they mean and how to respond to them, but after a few months of driving, your responses to road signs will be natural and automatic.

Debt

The last of the four wheels of the car that takes you to complete your home-buying journey is debt – or rather the knowledge of debts. In the world of finance, debt is perhaps the most important word of all. But for most first-time buyers, debt often conjures fear: the fear of being in debt. It's a burden. Because of that fear, many people would rather help their landlords pay off mortgage debts than take on their own debts.

It may be an honourable thought to live a life free of debt, especially a large debt. Without debt, one would be free as free as a bird – have you ever heard anyone say so? Yes, a bird may be free, but we are human beings living life in a modern world. We can never escape debt. Even the Queen of England has debt!

If you are an adult and you don't own a home, then you are always in debt in one way or another. Not having your own home, you would have to owe monthly rent to your landlord. You probably could claim that you are debt-free, if you were lucky enough to live with your parents and they didn't charge you rent – to a certain extent. On the other side of the spectrum of homeownership, you may have paid off your mortgage completely and think that you now don't own anyone a penny, but try to ignore the council tax bill when it arrives and you will know whether you are really debt-free or not. Therefore, debt is part of our modern life. Don't be scared of debt. Learn to live it with and use it for your own benefits.

Many years ago, a young couple, friends of ours, spoke to us about their intention to buy a home because they were tired of renting. With a ready deposit of £20,000, they looked at a house and liked it at a price around £150,000. However, despite our encouragement and sharing experience, they went away and did some sophisticated calculations and worked out that if they bought the house on a 25-year mortgage, by the time they paid off their mortgage, they would have paid more than £150,000 in interest to the bank. So, the total amount of interest they would have to pay is equivalent to the price of the house! The couple decided that it was not wise to be in debt for so long and to have to pay the bank so much in interest over 25 years. They showed the calculations to some people in their families who also advised them against getting into debts. Having a big mortgage over such a long time was a burden, they concluded.

But they still wanted to buy a house. To avoid the debt problem, they came up with a plan to save money until such a time that they could buy a house outright with cash in their bank account, not having to borrow money from a bank. We were, of course, impressed with their decision to buy a house and we admired their determination to save money and the discipline they were going to impose on themselves. And we asked them two questions. The first question was how much they could save a year. The couple, who both earned well above average salaries for their ages, thought every year they could set aside at least £8,000 after paying their rent and all the bills.

Our next question to them was what the price of the house would be when they had saved enough money to buy without a mortgage. They went and did some research and estimated conservatively that in the next ten years the price of the house they wanted to buy could almost double, so approximately £300,000. It then became quite clear that if they could discipline themselves and save for 10 years, they would have only £80,000. Optimistically, with their £20,000 saving and with some extra help from families, they could probably raise up to £150,000 after ten years. But by then, as they predicted, the house price would have been doubled. The truth is this story happened almost 20 years ago by the time this book was published. The couple changed their mind and took on a mortgage debt from a bank to buy the house, and it is now worth nearly £500,000 and they have paid off their mortgage. We hope you can work out the moral of the story.

Although debt has existed for almost as long as the history of human-kind, it's probably not until the turning of this millennium that it has been categorized into good debt and bad debt by Robert Kiyosaki, a well-known American real estate investor and writer, through his famous book *Rich Dad Poor Dad* (Kiyosaki, 2002) – at least, not in such simple terms as he discusses in the book.

As Kiyosaki (2002) suggests, there are good debts and bad debts. One should try to eliminate all the bad debts as fast as possible, but one should not be shy away from accumulating good debts to create wealth.

Bad debt

For Kiyosaki, a bad debt is the loan you borrow to buy a depreciating asset. In simple language, it is a loan you borrow to buy something that will lose value over time. If you borrow a loan to buy a new car at the price of £20,000, for instance, the moment you drive the car out of the dealership, your car has already lost some value. If you sold that car the next day, you would not get £20,000. The longer you use the car the less money you would get when you sell it. Unfortunately, there are so many things in our daily life that are necessary, but if we take out a loan to buy them, the loan becomes a bad debt. Just take a quick glance around yourself, you can see many of them: computer, fridge, furniture, mobile phones, etc. You would need to buy them out of necessity, but the advice is not to borrow money to buy them. Buy them when you can afford with your money. Yet, in certain circumstances, you may take out a loan to buy them, for instance, if you want to buy a van to run your delivery business. Or you may borrow some money to buy a high spec laptop to set up your graphic design business. In these cases, you borrow money to buy a depreciating asset, but the asset will produce a source of income, so it is no longer a bad debt. That bad debt becomes a good debt.

Good debt

On the contrary, a good debt is a loan you borrow to buy an asset which will increase in value – or in simple terms, buy something that you can sell later at a higher price. In another word, contrary to a bad debt, a good debt is a loan to buy an asset that will appreciate in value. Now, you may want to challenge the idea that buying a house is buying a good asset that will appreciate in value. For house prices can go up or go down. If the price of your house went up after you had bought it, then it would clearly be a good investment and the loan you had borrowed to buy it would be definitely a good debt. If the price of your house went down after you had bought it, then of course, the loan would be a bad debt. However, owning your home is a long-term project and the mortgage loan is normally spread over a couple of decades. So, in order to assess whether the house you buy will appreciate in value, you need to take a long-term view.

In the following chapters, we will show you how to minimise the risk of buying a house that depreciates in value. But you should appreciate it is a long journey. While house prices may go up or down in a short term, evidence has shown that in a peaceful country like the UK, you can expect house price on average to be doubled every 20 years, as can be seen in Figure 2.4.

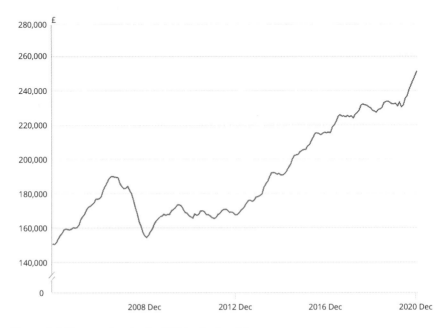

Figure 2.4 House prices in the UK in the last 20 years

Source: ONS (2021), 'UK House Price Index: December 2020'

The burden of mortgage payment

The other aspect of debts that frightens many people is not whether one should take on a debt but the interest on the debt and the ability to pay off the debt. While this fear is real because of the uncertainties one faces over a long period of time, determination and discipline – as we will show how in later chapters – will help allay this fear.

Once you have taken out a mortgage loan, you must make the monthly mortgage payments until you pay off the loan completely. Within the mortgage payment, there are two components: the loan amount (capital borrowed) and the interest which is the cost of borrowing money. Much will be discussed and analysed in later chapters, but for now, to prepare for your mindset, you can compare monthly mortgage payments with monthly rental payments.

Let's assume you take out a ten-year fixed-rate mortgage loan to buy a house and the monthly mortgage payment (which includes both interest and loan) is the same amount as your monthly rent. After the first ten years, your monthly payment amount will be significantly reduced. However, if you did not buy a house and continued to rent, your monthly rent would substantially be increased – at least by the rate of inflation. What's more, if the full life of the mortgage loan were 25 years, after 25 years you would own the house outright. But if you continued to pay rent for 25 years, guess who will own outright the house you stay in? You're right. Your landlord will.

In Chapter 8, we will look at mortgage debt in much more detail and will provide you with tools and strategies to manage it over however long you may require. But by now, hopefully, you have developed a growth 4-D mindset which will facilitate your learning in the coming chapters and prepare yourself for the journey to buy and own your first property.

References

Blackwell, L., Trzesniewski, K., and Dweck, C., 2007, 'Implicit Theories of Intelligence Predict Achievement Across an Adolescent Transition: A Longitudinal Study and an Intervention', *Child Development*, 78(1), pp. 246–263.

Connors, R., and Smith, T., 2002, *Journey to the Emerald City*. Paramus, NJ: Prentice Hall Press.

Dweck, C., 2007, *Mindset: The New Psychology of Success*. New York: Ballantine Books.

Kiyosaki, R., 2002 *Rich Dad Poor Dad: What the Rich Teach Their Kids About Money That the Poor and Middle Class Do Not*! London: Time Warner Books.

McCarty, W., 2002, 'The Power of Beliefs: What Babies Are Teaching Us', *Journal of Prenatal & Perinatal Psychology & Health*, 16(4), pp. 341–360.

ONS (2021), 'UK House Price Index: December 2020'. Available at https://www.ons.gov.uk/economy/inflationandpriceindices/bulletins/housepriceindex/december2020.

CHAPTER THREE
THE HOUSE-BUYING PROCESS

Buying a house is stressful, because many things can go wrong on the way. In England and Wales, the level of stress is greater because there is no legal commitment until contracts are exchanged, and the buyer and the seller face a lot of uncertainty as either party can change their mind at any time up to that point. The buyer has to spend money on various fees with no guarantee that they will own the property, while the seller faces a daunting prospect that the buyer might pull out from the sale, through either a change of heart or inability to get a mortgage, and spoil their plans.

While some buyers are lucky to go through the purchase smoothly, others might face numerous problems in the process and experience long delays. Indeed, the formal process of buying a property can be a drawn-out process, and might take anywhere between six weeks and eight months or longer.

The purpose of this chapter is to outline the key stages in the process of buying a house, so that you know what you need to do if any problems arise.

The process of buying a house

The process of buying a house involves seven key steps, as shown in Figure 3.1. Unlike Scotland, there is no legal commitment to buy or sell in England and Wales until step 6 when contracts are exchanged

Figure 3.1 The process of buying a property

(see MoneySavingExpert and Money Advice Service for more details). Until that point, both buyers and sellers can change their mind, creating a lot of uncertainty. We will now discuss the process and the potential issues that might arise in each stage in some detail.

Step 1: The decision to buy and make necessary preparations

Although the formal process of buying a property might take anywhere from six weeks to a few months, in reality the process takes much longer. This is because the process really begins in your mind when you decide that you are ready to embark on a journey to buy a property.

Once this decision is made, there are five preparations you need to make:

1 **Organize finance**: You might want to organize your finances, save for a deposit and upfront costs, and think about who to buy with, where and what to buy.
2 **Check your credit profile**: When you apply for a mortgage, a lender checks your credit profile to establish whether you will be a reliable borrower based on your previous financial transactions.

Rather than finding out the problems when you submit your mortgage application, it might be useful to check your profile to make sure that there are no errors or inaccuracies and that you have a good credit history. You can order a report from a credit referencing agency, such as Experian (www.experian.co.uk), and see what is recorded on there.

3 **Find out how much you can borrow**: This is important because it will determine whether you can buy on your own, who you buy with, where and what you can afford to buy, and it will give you confidence when you begin negotiation.

There are two ways you find out how much you can borrow. You can use a mortgage affordability calculator available from the Money Advice Service or go a lender's website. Most lenders have a mortgage calculator to enable you to find out how much you can borrow by inputting information about your income and financial commitments.

However, this can only serve as a rough guide of the amount you can borrow, because a mortgage calculator does not factor in your credit score and so the amount you can borrow can change.

4 **Speak to a mortgage adviser**: It is advisable to speak to a good independent mortgage adviser about your situation and explore options. They can research the market and then advise you of the different options available. We have always regretted not following a friend's recommendation to speak to a mortgage adviser when we were looking to buy our first property.

Some independent mortgage advisers charge a fee; others do not because they offset the commission they receive from a lender against the cost. You can find a mortgage adviser from www.unbiased.co.uk.

5 **Find a good solicitor to do the legal work**: It might be advisable to begin thinking about which solicitor (also known as conveyancer) you want to use and get an estimate of their fees. Having a solicitor will help you with negotiation as this shows you are a serious buyer.

Step 2: Find a property

Once you know roughly how much you can borrow, you can begin your property search. In the old days, peering through an estate agent's windows was a common way to see what your money can get you in the area you want to buy.

Now, you can do a property search anywhere in the world using your phone, computer or iPad. A disadvantage with this is that anyone can now view the property anywhere in the world too, and buyers can come from around the globe. This can potentially increase competition and price.

Use the right property finding sites

There is a plethora of property search websites you can use to find a property, including Rightmove, Zoopla, On the Market, and Home. These websites save you a lot of time and provide you with information to help you decide whether the property is suitable.

These websites can tell you a lot of valuable information, including:

- Floor layout, description the property, room sizes
- How long has the property been on the market? This helps you establish whether the property you want to buy stay around for a while, or get snapped up. This gives you some indication of its desirability. If a property has been on the market for a long time, this means that there is low interest and might put you in a stronger negotiating position.
- What other similar properties are selling for? This tells you whether the property is over-priced or not, or whether there is a glut of similar properties in the same area. If there are many similar properties on the market, it might suggest some problems with the area.

  This also tells you whether there is a steady supply of the type of home you are thinking of buying, or whether they are few or far between.
- How much the seller bought the property for? This tells you whether the seller has made a profit or loss, and this information can help you with negotiation.

  You can now find out the price of a property using various sites, such as Nethouseprices, Zoopla and Land Registry.
- How many agents are selling the same property? Sellers who are desperate often instruct several agents at the same time. If the property is listed with several estate agents, it indicates that the

seller needs to move quickly and so you can enhance your negotiating position by emphasizing the speed you can complete the purchase.

- Property alerts: you can register your details with different sites so that you will receive notifications when a new property comes on the market.

    However, looking at a property on a website is no substitute for a physical viewing. In fact, photos on the website can be misleading and do not tell you about the neighbourhood and surrounding areas. You need to go and view an interested property as soon as possible before other buyers get there.

Speak to your local estate agent

Some homes are sold before they appear online. This is because estate agents have a list of registered buyers on their database. It is therefore important that you get to know local estate agents and tell them what type of property you are looking for and your budget. They should be able to give you an idea of how realistic it is, how many other buyers you could expect to be up against and how long it is taking on average for that type of property to sell.

You can register your details with them and receive notifications when new properties come onto the market. It is worthwhile to keep in touch with estate agents and give them a call on a regular basis so that you can strengthen the relationship and ensure that they keep you in mind when the next suitable property comes up.

Check out the neighbourhood

You need to do a lot of research on your chosen area and find out about the following aspects.

1 **Noise**: You can use this website to check the noise and air quality level: www.extrium.co.uk/noiseviewer.html.
2 **Future development proposals**: Are there upcoming planning proposals which will change the area – for better or worse?

For England and Wales, the Government's planning portal (see Planning Portal) helps avoid nasty surprises by directing you to planning applications made in your area. You can search by post-code and area.

3   **Crime**: Police crime-mapping websites (see Police UK) show local hotspots and break down recorded crimes such as burglary and anti-social behaviour.
4   **School**: The government's school league tables (Gov.UK) list all schools in your local area, provide information about each school and its Ofsted rating, and compare student performance with the average in the local authority and nationally.
5   **Flood risk:** Flood risk has a significant impact on insurance premiums, a property's value and your quality of life. It is therefore important that you check the risk of flooding using the following websites:

The Environment Agency (England and Wales) and Environment Protection Agency's (Scotland) provide detailed reports on whether and why an area is at risk of flooding.

Tip: careful who you buy a property from

A young man found a flat in north London and was offered a price half of its market value. He paid the 'selling agent' a £5,000 deposit for each flat and recommended several friends to do the same.

His mortgage adviser submitted his mortgage application but the surveyor could not obtain access to the property to value it. He went to search for the 'selling agent', only to find that she had no right to sell the property and had disappeared with all the deposit money she had taken from him and his friends.

Step 3: Put in an offer

Once you decide you want to buy the property, you need to make an offer.

The asking price gives you some indication of what the seller wants. Depending on the market conditions and how many other buyers want the same property, you can put in an offer below the asking price or pay the full asking price. Chapter 5 provides some tips on how to negotiate the price.

If the property is in high demand, making an offer well below the asking price puts you at risk of being gazumped (the seller changes his or her mind and sells to someone else for a higher price) or gazanged (a seller pulls out of a property transaction). It is important to remember that estate agents may continue to advertise the house and show it to other prospective buyers until the contract is exchanged between the buyer and the seller.

Risks after an offer accepted include:

- Gazumping – seller sells to another buyer for a higher price after accepting your offer
- Gazanging – seller decides not to sell

Step 4: Apply for a mortgage

Once you have found a property, you need to apply for a mortgage. Sometimes an estate agent wants you to provide a decision in principle (DIP), also known as agreement in principle (AIP), before you view a property to show that you can get a mortgage. However, applying for a decision in principle can leave a footprint on your credit profile, and if you have too many applications done, this can affect your credit score and reduce your ability to get a mortgage. It is therefore better to apply for a decision in principle once you have agreed the price.

Case study: A young couple struggled to get a mortgage. As they had six to seven mortgage applications submitted in one month, their credit score declined with each application. After their last mortgage application was submitted, the lender wrote to their mortgage adviser to ask why they had submitted so many applications. Their adviser explained that their inexperience and great desire to buy the property made them act in haste. The lender accepted the explanation and offered them a mortgage. This example shows that an adviser can add value and help secure a mortgage.

Once the DIP (or AIP) is done, the next step is to convert it to a full application, when you need to submit full details about the property and your personal circumstances (e.g. employment details). Before a lender can issue a mortgage offer, they will need to carry out a mortgage valuation on the property. This will be discussed in more detail in Chapter 8.

Potential problems with valuation

When a surveyor carries out a valuation on a property, a few potential problems can arise, especially if you are buying an older property.

1   **Down valuation**: A surveyor might value a property less than the price you have agreed to pay. If this is the case, it will affect the amount you can borrow.

For example: you agree to buy a property at £100,000 but a surveyor values the property at £95,000. This means that the agreed price is £5,000 more than the value.

This down-valuation affects how much you can borrow. Imagine you apply for a 90 per cent mortgage and if the property is worth £100,000, you can borrow £90,000. However, the property is now worth £95,000, a 90 per cent mortgage means you can only borrow £85,500. There are three potential solutions to deal with this problem

1 find the extra amount of money
2 ask the vendor to reduce the price
3 apply for a mortgage with a different lender, whose surveyor might not down-value the property.

2   **Retention**: If the mortgage valuation report identifies any issues with the property, a mortgage lender might decide to keep back some of the money until the works are done (known as retention).

For example: a property might need a new bathroom or kitchen. A lender might decide to keep an amount of money (equivalent to the cost of replacement those items). This can cause problems, particularly if the retained amount is significant, because you will need to find more money in order to complete the purchase of the property.

There are two potential solutions:

1 One solution is to change the lender, who might instruct a different surveyor and who might have a different opinion on the property. However, you might have to incur a fee for this.
2 You can also go back to the vendor and renegotiate the price.

3 **Problems with the property**: A survey might highlight problems with the property, such as subsistence and damp. Read the survey report carefully and get a quote for the works and then go back to re-negotiate the price. Some buyers might walk away because the cost of repairs might be too high and they may not have the money to pay for these.

Step 5: Instruct solicitor

Conveyancing is the legal process that transfers a property from one person to another. Licensed conveyancers are specialist property lawyers/ solicitors, who do all the legal paperwork, Land Registry and local council searches, draft the contract and handle the exchange of money.

Conveyancers or solicitors carry out several important searches on the property:

1 **Local authority searches**: Check to see if there is anything you need to be aware of, such as any building control issues, enforcement actions and nearby road schemes.

Case study: A young couple instructed a solicitor to carry out a local authority search for their proposed property. The search found that there was a plan to use the rail-line at the back of the garden for freight train.

The couple was worried that the noise level may affect the re-sale value of the property and so decided to pull out from the sale, after having paid £1,500 for a full structural survey and a few hundred pounds in legal fees.

2 **Drainage searches**: Check it is connected to sewers.
3 **Environmental search**: Check the land is not contaminated.

Step 6: Exchange contracts

Transfer money to pay for the deposit

Before you exchange contracts, you need to transfer money to pay for the deposit. Most banks do not usually allow you to move more than £25,000 out of an account per day, so if you want to move more than this, you will need to call your bank and arrange a CHAPS payment to your solicitor.

A CHAPS payment (it stands for Clearing House Automated Payment System) is usually made the same day. You'll need to pay your bank between £20 and £35 per CHAPS payment.

Your solicitor will also get you to sign the contract at this point – this is the point where you commit to buying the seller's house.

There is now a legally binding contract between you and the seller. Once this has happened, you cannot pull out from the sale. If you do, you will forfeit your deposit money. But, on the plus side, the seller cannot back out either.

Tip: do not agree an exchange date until you have a mortgage in place

Some people may agree an exchange date when they agree the price and before they receive a mortgage offer. It is best to avoid this because a mortgage offer might take longer than expected and a delay in exchange might involve paying a heavy financial penalty.

Buildings insurance

You might not own your property yet, but once you have exchanged contracts you are legally bound to purchase it, so you need to have buildings insurance in place.

Some insurance companies base their price on a specific rebuild value (this is stated in the valuation report) and on an unlimited rebuild cost.

Life insurance/health insurance/unemployment in place

After exchange you are legally bound to buy the property, and therefore it is worthwhile to take out life and health insurance and unemployment cover.

Case study: A young buyer was excited to move into her property. She collected the keys but died unexpectedly on the day she moved into her home.

Step 7: Completion

After you exchange contracts, you need to prepare for completing the purchase of the property.

Negotiate a completion date

Your solicitor will update you on the results of the searches. If all is good, the next step is to come to an agreement on a completion date with the seller. The completion date is the date the keys get handed over. This needs to be a date that suits both you and the seller.

Get a completion statement from your solicitor

Your solicitor will give you a completion statement with a clear break-down of the money you need to give the solicitor. This will include any outstanding deposit, stamp duty land tax, solicitors' fees, etc. You'll usually have to pay these on or before your completion date.

If you intend to pay for some of the costs using your LISA funds, you need to let your solicitor know.

Your solicitor will carry out more searches

Before completion, your solicitor has to check that the seller still owns the property and that you haven't been made bankrupt since your mortgage offer.

You need to sign the transfer deed

Your solicitor will prepare the transfer deed. You need to sign it, and it needs to be witnessed. It confirms you're willing to take ownership of the property. Your solicitor will send it to the seller's solicitor.

Your solicitor draws down the funds from your lender

Your solicitor will request the mortgage money from your lender so that payment has time to clear in the solicitor's account. It is at this point you (your solicitor) actually get the mortgage money you've agreed to borrow.

Paying for the house

The solicitor will send the full payment to the seller's solicitor and receive their title deeds and proof that the seller's mortgage has been cleared (this means their bank no longer has a claim on the property).

Pay your stamp duty (through your solicitor)

In theory, you have 14 days for your solicitor to send the Stamp Office your transfer deed and your stamp duty land tax payment. In practice, solicitors normally ask for you to send this payment before they can complete the purchase for you.

However, as a first-time buyer, you are exempt from stamp duty if the price of your property is below a certain level.

Officially register your ownership

Your solicitor will register your details with the Land Registry. You will need to send them a fee to cover this. Again, this is usually detailed in the statement of completion and paid on the day of completion.

Your solicitor will get the new title deeds from the Land Registry and forward them to your mortgage lender (or you if you're mortgage-free). Sometimes they'll keep them on file if you don't request them, or don't want to keep such important documents in the house.

Potential problems after exchange:

1   **Death of seller**

After you exchange contracts, there might be delays to completion. These delays could be due to the inability of the seller (usually builders) to finish the works in time for completion, or by events such as death of the seller.

Case study: A young couple paid a 10 per cent deposit and exchanged contracts for their property purchase. They also gave notice on their rental flat. However, the seller died after contracts were exchanged, resulting in delays as the estate of the seller had to go to probate.[1] Luckily, the solicitor was able to secure an order which allowed the couple to move in before completion.

2   **Fall in property price as a result of long delay between exchange and completion**

When you buy a new build property, especially an off-plan property, sometimes there is a long time-lag between exchange and completion.

A mortgage offer, however, is normally valid for six months, and means that you might face a risk of a fall in property price.

In 2008, many people experienced this problem, especially those who bought a new build property from builders. It is possible to obtain a mortgage on a property which is not being built, but a lender usually requires an inspection when the building is completed. However, as there is a long time-lag between the time when a mortgage offer is issued and the building work completed, house prices could fall, as was the case in 2008. When the builder refused to reduce the price, buyers had to walk away from their deal as they were unable to borrow the amount needed and lost a 5 per cent deposit as a consequence. One way to reduce this risk is to buy a property which is close to completion to reduce the time-lag and avoid the risk of a downturn in the market.

3   **Your circumstances as a buyer could change preventing you from proceeding – loss of a job, relationship break up**

After exchange a buyer might experience a change in circumstances – losing job or experiencing a relationship break-up. Some buyers might have to pull out from the deal and lose the deposit. Having a financial buffer can help you deal with the unexpected.

In short, the house-buying process is filled with uncertainties and risks, and ownership is not guaranteed until you collect the keys on the day of completion. It is important to be aware of the risks so that you can take appropriate action to mitigate these.

Summary

After outlining the process of buying a house, we will now turn to the crucial question of where and what type of property you should buy.

Note

1   **Probate** is the process of administering a deceased person's estate. This involves organizing their money, assets and possessions and distributing them as inheritance after paying any taxes and debts.

References

Gov.UK, *Search for Schools and Colleges to Compare* [online]. Available at www. compare-school-performance.service.gov.uk [Accessed 12 November 2020].

The Money Advice Service, *Mortgage Affordability Calculator – How Much Mortgage Can You Afford to Borrow?* [online]. Available at www.money adviceservice.org.uk/en/tools/house-buying/mortgage-affordability-calculator [Accessed 12 November 2020].

The Money Advice Service, *Home-Buying Process – Steps to Buying a New House or Flat* [online]. Available at www.moneyadviceservice.org.uk/en/articles/ money-timeline-when-buying-property-england-wales-n-ireland [Accessed 12 November 2020].

MoneySavingExpert, *Buying a Home – The Timeline* [online]. Available at www. moneysavingexpert.com/mortgages/buying-a-home-timeline [Accessed 12 November 2020].

Planning Portal, *Find Your LPA* [online]. Available at https://1app.planningportal. co.uk/YourLpa/FindYourLpa [Accessed 12 November 2020].

Police UK, *Metropolitan Police Service* [online]. Available at www.police.uk/ pu/your-area/metropolitan-police-service [Accessed 12 November 2020].

Chapter Four
Where and what to buy

One of the most important decisions you have to make at the beginning of the process of buying a house is the question of **where** you want to buy, followed by the question of **what** kind of property you want to buy.

Choosing a right kind of property is important because it can affect your happiness, quality of life, overall well-being, resale value and your ability to sell in the future. Some properties are in great demand with buyers fighting over them, while others are unsaleable with no interest from potential buyers. Obviously, you want to buy a saleable property so that you can turn property into cash when needed.

The key is to buy a 'desirable' property. What makes a property desirable is determined by the location and the characteristics of the property. Location, however, always takes precedence and so you need to focus on this first before deciding on a specific property.

The aim of this chapter is to help you find the right kind of property by discussing the factors you need to consider in choosing a location and a property.

What makes a good location?

You may have heard the phrase "location, location and location" many times, or you may have come across the TV series which has that title presented by the property expert Kirstie Allsopp. If you haven't, then be prepared to hear it over and over, and repeat this until you have found the house you want to buy.

Although what makes a location or an area desirable can be subjective and may differ from one person to another, there are a few fundamental factors that affect the perception of a good location.

Identify the desirable area and buy close to it

One way to identify a good area to buy is to find the desirable area and buy as close to it as you can. In every town or city, there are areas which are seen to be very desirable to live in. The 'posh end of town' always commands a premium price over other areas. In London, for example, Chelsea and South Kensington will always be popular because the rich and wealthy want to live there.

These areas are desirable because they have better environment (wider roads and more green spaces), nice architecture and central location. Over time, the desirable areas become self-fulfilling. As people want to live there, businesses want to locate there. This means that the areas attract boutique shops, fine restaurants, good pubs and better facilities. As a result, competition for housing there might be high and so prices tend to be higher than other areas.

As a first-time buyer, the prices in the desirable areas might be beyond your reach. One strategy to find a balance between desirability and affordability is to follow a concentric ring model and look at areas outside the 'prime' area (i.e. desirable and popular). These areas are a good choice because they can benefit from the 'ripple effect' of the house price increases in the 'prime' area, as buyers who cannot afford the expensive areas move out to the zone where they can afford.

The importance of postcodes

It is vital that you do research on postcodes and find out the postcode of your property before you decide to buy it because postcodes affect desirability of a property and the cost of home and car insurance. In some parts of the country (e.g. London), the postcode can add or detract thousands of pounds to/from a property's value.

To complicate matters, the boundaries for postcodes can be one side of the street or the other. A property located in a very desirable postcode, even if it is on the boundary of the postcode, can command a higher price than an identical property across the road that falls into another postcode. You can use the following website to check the postcode: https://checkmypostcode.uk/.

7 criteria to help you choose

When you search for an area, you can use the following 7 criteria to guide you to choose the right one:

1 **Safety**: safe location with low crime
2 **Space**: a lot of open public space and the property is spacious
3 **Schools**: near good schools
4 **Supermarkets**: close to supermarkets
5 **Stations**: close to stations (railway station or Tube station)
6 **Sports and stadiums**: close to sports and football stadiums
7 **Special**: close to a good hospital, university, pub or water

Safety: low crime level

A key factor that affects the perception of a good and bad area is the level of crime, as the need for safety is the second most important human needs, after physiological needs (food, shelter, air, water).

We all want to live in areas where we can feel relatively safe. No one wants to live in areas where it is unsafe to walk around, where there are high incidences of vandalism, murder, rape, assaults and burglaries. The level of crime, therefore, is a key factor in affecting the desirability of an area. Research suggests that proximity to crime hotspots affects prices of houses for family more than prices of flats (Ceccato and Wilhelmsson, 2019).

There are websites where you can check the crime level of an area, such as: www.adt.co.uk/crime-in-my-area.

Space: open green space and spacious property

Many people like to live in areas with a lot of public open space (e.g. parks) because these improve the quality of life and enhance individual well-being by providing space for daily leisure, recreation and aesthetic enjoyment.

Research shows that public urban green spaces can increase a terrace property value by 42 per cent and apartment by 49 per cent (McCord et al., 2014).

Schools

Living in a catchment area of a good school is important for families with children because school admission rules are mainly based on location. Proximity to a good school has a huge effect on property values.

Research by Confused.com shows that demand for secondary school places has increased significantly over the past five years due to high birth rates in the early 2000s (Confused, The School Catchment Crisis, 2019). Demand is now outstripping supply. In 2013–14, just under half a million pupils applied for secondary schools. This increased to more than 560,000 in 2017/18 and the number of secondary school pupils is expected to rise by a further 540,000 between 2017 and 2025.

House prices in areas with an outstanding Ofsted rating are reported to cost nearly £100,000 more than areas with 'inadequate' rating. However, there is a huge regional variation. In 2019, the most expensive postcode for an 'outstanding' school in London was SW7, where the average price was nearly £1.8 million. Houses near an 'outstanding' school in Birmingham cost £248,000. Sunderland was the cheapest place where areas near an 'outstanding' school cost £114,000 (Confused, 2019).

While you may not have children and need to be close to a good school, living near one can affect how much you can sell your property for in the future.

Supermarkets

Having a supermarket within walking distance can influence the value of a property because it offers convenience and saves time. It is believed that proximity to high-end supermarkets (such as Waitrose) increases property value by 15 per cent, but for London properties, studies show that having a premium brand on your doorstep is likely to increase your property value by 50 per cent.

In 2017, the *Independent* reported that the "Waitrose effect" can add over £36,000 to a property price typically, while proximity to Marks and Spencer increases a property value by almost £30,000, and to a national supermarket by around £22,000 (Independent, 2017).

In the past five years, proximity to budget supermarkets (including Aldi, Asda, Lidl, Tesco and Morrisons) has increased property value on average by 15 per cent (Johns&Co, 2020).

Stations: train/Tube station/bus

Everyone likes convenience. Proximity to stations saves commuting time, parking costs and stress as you have control over travelling time. For example, if you live near a train station, you can walk there and do not pay for parking. Walking provides daily exercise and also reduces stress as you do not need to worry about finding a parking space. Areas near a train station therefore are often desirable for this reason.

If you live in London, for example, being close to a Tube station is important as many people do not have cars. Research by Nationwide shows that properties 500 m from a Tube station carry a 10.5 per cent premium compared to those a kilometre further away. That translates to an extra £54,021 above the average London property price. In other towns such as Glasgow and Manchester, properties 500 m from a station attract a 6 per cent premium and 4.6 per cent, respectively, compared to those further away (Struttandparker.com, 2018).

Sports and stadiums

The building or redevelopment of a major sporting stadium appears to have a huge impact on house prices.

One of the UK's biggest developments in recent years is the creation of the Queen Elizabeth Olympic Park, a sporting complex in Stratford, East London. Built for the 2012 Olympics, the park included an athletes' Olympic village, several sporting buildings (the London Stadium and London Aquatics Centre), an observation tower (which is now Britain's largest piece of public art) and Westfield Shopping Centre.

This development had a significant impact on house prices. The Halifax reported that property for sale in Stratford, especially the houses in postal districts near to the London Olympic stadium, increased by 64 per cent from £286,683 to £470,487, which is an average of £4,279 per month between September 2012 and April 2017.

The Halifax also looked at the impact of stadiums in other areas. It compared house prices near past and present Premier League teams over the last 20 years and found that in comparison to a national average increase of 247 per cent, prices in these locations increased at a much higher rate. Prices near Portsmouth Club rose at the lowest rate, by 276 per cent, while property prices near Tottenham Hotspur grew at the highest level, by 655 per cent (Lee, 2018).

Living close to a famous sporting venue can also make a big difference to the property. Areas in London such as Wimbledon, Wembley, Twickenham and Stratford can command up to 10 per cent more than neighbouring boroughs because they have a great arena nearby.

Furthermore, living close to a popular sporting venue also gives you an opportunity to earn an extra income by renting out driveway or parking when there are big events on. In places such as Wimbledon, short-term lets during the tennis championship can generate a significant amount of rental income (Pettyson, 2020).

Special: does the area have special features?

Good hospitals

Proximity to a good hospital has a significant impact on house prices. Many homeowners feel more comfortable knowing that a hospital is nearby, just in case something should go wrong. It is also of vital importance for those with ongoing or unique healthcare needs requiring specialist assistance on a more regular basis.

House prices in areas in England with a nearby hospital increase faster than the national average (Jones, 2017). According to Emoov, the average house price near the UK's top ten hospitals was slightly over £350,000 in 2017, which was significantly higher than the national house price average of £231,000. Areas with the top hospitals saw an average house price increase of 45 per cent, which was 11 per cent more than England as a whole. Hospitals clearly have an impact on house prices (Emoov, 2017).

Again, there is a huge regional variation. The most affordable area where the average house price with outstanding hospitals can be found is the North West, with an average house price of £130,000 in 2017 (Jones, 2017). However, prices have increased significantly. By May 2021, the average price of a property in North West England has increased to £209,000 (Zoopla, 2021). The East of England, on the other hand, has high property prices but poor hospitals. Hemel Hempstead General Hospital, for example, is rated as inadequate, but its average house price in 2017 was £405,653. By May 2021, this has fallen to £396,000 (Zoopla, 2021).

Good universities

The best universities tend to enhance local property values because they encourage inward business investment and start-ups. In addition, parents may want to buy in the area for their children. Research shows that owning a home in a city with a top university could add an extra £28,724 to the price of your property (What Mortgage, 2020).

One way to identify a good university is to look at the Russell Group Universities. These make up 24 red brick universities and support 261,000 jobs. They generate nearly £87 billions for the UK economy. In 2018–19, they had more than 446,000 undergraduates and 155,000 postgraduates studying in them (Russell Group; Alegre-Wood 2017).

Good pubs

Some buyers want to be close to a good local pub. Close proximity to a good pub is believed to add as much as 10 per cent to property prices (Pettyson, 2020; Pollara, 2020).

Close to Water

Areas near water are always desirable because there are a limited number of properties that can be located near it. Properties with water views will always be in higher demand than those without, as people like looking out at water. It is also aesthetically pleasing and means that you are not going to be overlooked by other buildings. However, issues such as coastal erosion and flooding will need to be investigated.

It is believed that if you can also secure fishing rights, this can increase the house value by 15 per cent (Pettyson, 2020).

What factors are important to you?

To help you choose the right kind of location, it might be worthwhile to construct a personal matrix so that you can see what is important to you, shown in Table 4.1. For each factor, you can rate on the scale of 1 to 5.

How to get to know an area?

If you do not know the area you are intending to buy in, it is well worth spending some time to get to know the area. Ideally, you should visit the area at least three times, once on a weekday, once at night and once at a weekend.

Table 4.1 Factors important to you

Factors	1. Not very important	2. Not important	3. Neutral	4. Important	5. Very important
Safety					
Space					
Schools					
Supermarkets					
Stations					
Sports/stadiums					
Special features					
Hospital					
University					
Pub					
Water					

Some apparently quiet areas might be inflicted by problems such as commuter traffic during the rush hour or gangs of marauding youths after dark.

Here are some other useful ways to assess an area:

Visit

- *Local shops*: Do they sell the sort of things you want to buy?
- *Local pubs*: Do you feel at home with the locals?
- *Local parks*: Are they clean and well kept?

Speak

- *Local shop owners*: You can get a lot of useful information from local shop owners, as they can tell you what the area is like and how well the business is doing.
- *Local estate agents*: Speaking to a local estate agent will give you a good insight into an area. You can ask them about what types of people look for property in this area, which road/street is desirable and in demand.
- *People who live in the area*: The people who live in the area can tell you what is like to live there and the problems to expect.

Check out

- *Local transport*: Try doing the journey to work to see what is like to commute.

Observe

- *Gardens*: Are they well-maintained?
- *Number of bells on each door*: More than one means that the house has been converted into flats. This could cause noise and parking problems.
- *Look through the windows*: The curtains, décor and furnishings will give you a good idea of the age and background of the people who live there.
- *Skips/conversions*: Look at the number of skips and conversions in the area. This can tell you whether the area is in high demand and people are maximising living space rather than move to another area.

What is the right type of property to buy?

Having chosen a good location or good area, the next step is to find the right property. While affordability is a fairly obvious factor, there are many other important factors that you need to take into account, including the ease of getting a mortgage. If you buy a property that you can get a mortgage from most lenders, you avoid paying high interest rates and expensive insurance.

Standard construction

Lenders prefer property of standard construction over non-standard. Standard construction means the property is normally built with brick or stone, and the roof is made of slate or tile. A non-standard construction is therefore anything that falls outside of this, and includes timber framed houses, log-style cabins and prefabricated concrete houses.

It is possible to get a mortgage on non-standard properties but you might need to approach a specialist lender. The consumer magazine *Which* (Which, 2019) has identified 16 different types of property which is more difficult to obtain a mortgage including:

- ex local authority housing – especially high-rise flats,
- properties made of concrete,
- flats above a shop or commercial premise,
- properties with annexes,
- multi-unit blocks,
- live/work units,
- studio flats,

- new build or recently renovated properties,
- properties with agricultural ties,
- freehold flats, properties with flying freehold,
- flats with no property management company,
- properties with short leases,
- properties not in a habitable condition,
- and eco-homes.

As non-standard construction properties carry a greater risk, lenders often charge a higher interest rate and restrict the loan-to-value to ensure that the mortgage does not exceed the value of the property. For these reasons, it is advisable to buy a standard property as it is easier to re-sell due to the ease of getting a mortgage.

Houses versus flats/apartments

Houses

The ideal type of property is houses because they are largely freehold and therefore you own the land on which the property stands. As the UK is an island country, the amount of land available is limited and valuable. They also offer the potential to enhance the value of the property by adding a conservatory and an extension, or converting the loft.

Detached properties are probably most desirable because they are not connected to any property, and therefore offer you more privacy and reduce the potential of conflict with neighbours. They might have a garden and parking space. They tend to hold their value better than other types of property.

However, detached properties might not be affordable or available in your chosen area. If this is the case, you might wish to look at the next best, such as semi-detached houses and then terraced houses.

Flats/apartments

For most first-time buyers, particularly in big cities, this category might be more desirable, because not only are flats more affordable, but they are often close to the city centre which give many social benefits. A flat, whether in a multi-storey block or a converted house, would certainly make a good first step on the housing ladder.

When all the conditions are right and favourable to you, it's often better to buy a flat in a good location than to wait until you can afford to buy a house with a garden somewhere else. For a decent flat in a good location will be easier to sell, should you need to move somewhere else or buy a bigger house. In a good location, flats tend to retain their long-term value, if not increase.

The drawbacks with most flats are often as follows:

- Leasehold: this means someone else owns the land, and you might have to pay ground rent.
- Maintenance and management and service fees.
- Restrictions from freeholder.
- Parking restrictions.

There are many flats which claim to have a "share of freehold". While these "share of freehold' flats may have fewer restrictions than a leasehold flat, they nevertheless pose some risks that you need to be aware of.

In January 2021, the government announced a significant leasehold reform. Under current rules, leaseholders of houses can only extend their lease once for 50 years with a ground rent, while leaseholders of flats can extend as often as they wish at a zero 'peppercorn' ground rent for 90 years. The new legislation means that both house and flat leaseholders will now be able to extend their lease to a new standard 990 years with a ground rent at zero. Millions of leaseholders will be able to benefit from this (Jones, 2021).

New-build versus second-hand properties

In some towns and cities, you might have a choice of new-build or second-hand properties in the area you have chosen. Many first-time buyers are attracted to new-build properties because these come with modern facilities. As they are new, you do not need to carry out any repairs/improvements before you can move in, and this reduces the burden of finding extra money. They also offer a ten-year warranty and you might also be able to choose the finishing touches (e.g. type of flooring, choice of paint). The builders might offer you incentives such as a contribution towards your deposit and legal costs. You can also take advantage of government incentives which can only be used on new-build property (e.g. Help to Buy Equity Loan discussed in Chapter 6).

However, new-build properties tend to be more expensive than a second-hand property, as there is a new-build premium. Once you have moved into the property, you will lose this premium and so the value of the property might go down.

Second-hand properties might be less desirable because the property might be old and does not have modern facilities (e.g. modern kitchen and bathroom). However, they might be cheaper and have a more central location, offering more convenience to public transport.

Freehold versus leasehold

Houses tend to be freehold, while flats/apartments leasehold. Freehold tends to be better because you own the land, and leasehold means you have to pay ground rent as someone owns the land.

As you own the land, you have the freedom to carry out improvements (such as build a conservatory or extension), whereas in a leasehold property you need permission from the landlord before any works can be carried out.

Property's characteristics

Uniqueness

A property with a special feature is desirable because it is scarce. A house in a road with a hundred identical properties will never really excite a buyer because they know that if they lose this property, there will be another one. A more unique property, on the other hand, generates more excitement because buyers know that if they miss it they will never find one like it.

Features to look out for include unusual window or fireplace, an aga or room size or size of garden.

Parking

Availability of parking is important and this is believed to add £50,000 to the price in some parts of the country (Pettyson, 2020).

Tree-lined street

Residential streets with trees separating the road and the pavement are more desirable than those lacking such luxury. These features can increase a property value by a few thousand pounds (Pettyson, 2020).

Importance of condition

The condition of the property affects its value. We live in a world where people seem to have less and less time and many buyers will not even consider a property that is in poor condition. However, you should not be put off by a property in a poor condition.

In fact, it is sometimes good if the property is in a poor condition because it is less desirable and therefore attracts less competition. If there is less competition, the seller is in a weaker bargaining position, allowing you to negotiate and get a better price. If you have time and imagination, you can buy properties in poor condition at a bargain.

Some aspects of the condition can easily be changed, such as colour of wall paint or type of flooring, with minimal costs. If the property requires a new bathroom or kitchen, this will involve a greater investment but you can carry out the works in stages.

Layout of the property

The layout of the property is quite important because it affects the use and enjoyment. The floor plan gives you an overview of the property. There are a few things to look out for when you look at the floor plan:

Lounge: Is it separate or connected to the kitchen/dining room?

Kitchen: Is it big enough to accommodate a small dining table? This is attractive if there is only reception room.

Size of the smallest bedroom: The minimum size has to be 6 feet 6 inches to get a bed in, otherwise it will be classified as a study or baby's room or nursery.

Bathroom: A bathroom is more desirable if there is a power shower. If there are two bathrooms, then the property is more desirable even though one may only be a shower room.

Electrics: Are the electric sockets old? Does the whole electrical system need re-wiring?

Heating: Is the heating system old? This can be costly to replace.

Garden: Which room opens out to the garden? Living room or kitchen?

Garage: Is the garage separate from the house, or linked? If it is linked, it might not require planning permission if you wish to convert it into a bedroom.

However, the layout can be changed, such as knocking down an internal wall, putting in an ensuite shower, modifying the layout of a kitchen and bathroom, and converting the loft and garage. This helps increase the value of your property but requires investment in time and cash.

Table 4.2 Assessing property

Features	Size (rate on scale 1–5)	Condition (rate on scale 1–5)	Repairs required (rate on scale of 1–5)	Potential for extension	General observations
Living room					
Dining room					
Kitchen					
Bathroom					
Shower					
Ensuite					
Bedroom 1					
Bedroom 2					
Bedroom 3					
Garden					
Downstairs cloakroom					
Separate toilet					
Heating					
Boiler					
Smallest room					Needs to be bigger than 6ft 6'
Electrics					
Service charge					
Garage					
Windows					
Roof					
Driveway					
Parking					

Other desirable features of a property

Property prices are affected not only by the number of bedrooms in a home but also by other features such as whether the home has a garage, driveway or loft, and how big the garden is. If the property has not got any of these additional features, you might want to think of its potential. Is there potential to add value to a property?

Regional differences in prices in the UK

One way to get on the property ladder is buy where prices are afford-able. The average house price in the UK was £247,000 in January 2020 but the average price in London is double this, surpassing £500,000 in January 2021. However, this is only an average price, and there are many areas within London with a lower price tag.

Living outside London is undoubtedly cheaper. The North of England is believed to be the most affordable region for first-time buyers. Although earnings are usually lower, house prices in the North are lower too. In January 2020, the average price for the North East was £127,000, in comparison to £140,000 for Northern Ireland, £152,000 for Scotland, £162,000 for Wales, £165,000 for North West, £195,000 East Midlands and £200,000 West Midland, as can be seen in Figure 4.1.

The average price in Birmingham was £206,000 in early 2021 (Zoopla, 2021). The city is popular because it has great transport links and good employment opportunities as it is a destination of choice for major companies, including the Big Four – PwC, KPMG, Deloitte and EY – which all have their largest regional offices based in the city. Big name banks also make Birmingham their home, and HSBC, Deutsche Bank, Metro Bank and Secure Trust Bank have all invested in the city in recent years (Cotton, 2019).

However, it is important to bear in mind that price is only one factor affecting our choice of where to buy a house. Other factors such as proximity to friends, family, relatives, work, countryside or the sea can play an equally crucial part. To ensure that you will be happy in your choice, it is advisable to focus first on finding out where you want to live and settle.

Summary

Your decision of where and what property to buy is very important because it can affect whether you will be happy living there, the potential increase in value and the ease of selling the property in the future.

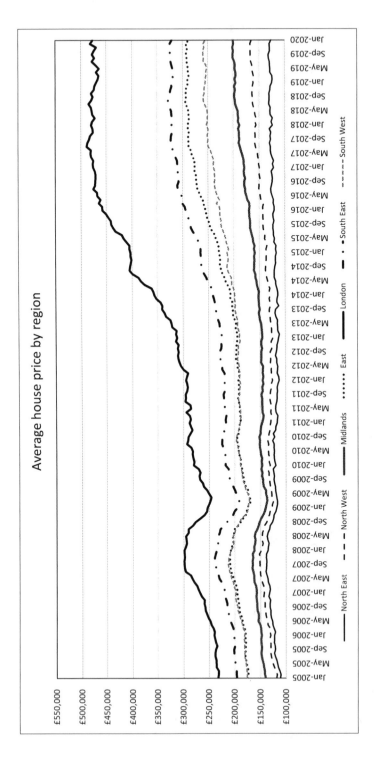

Figure 4.1 Regional differences in price

Source: UK House Price Index – Office for National Statistics (2020)

Research is the key to help you with this important decision. You need to do a lot of research and view as many properties as you can. By viewing many properties and taking a lot of notes, you can understand what is available and what you like. Once you have found a suitable property, you will need to know what to do to get the best price. We will discuss negotiation skills in the next chapter.

References

Alegre-Wood, B., 2017, 'Seven Reasons Why Investors Profit Near Universities', *Gladfish Property* [online]. Available at www.gladfish.com/the-benefits-of-investing-in-property-in-university-towns/ [Accessed 14 November 2020].

Ceccato, V., and Wilhelmsson, M., 2019, 'Do Crime Hot Spots Affect Housing Prices?', *Nordic Journal of Criminology*, 21(1), pp. 84–102.

Confused.com, 2019, *The School Catchment Crisis: How High Ofsted Ratings Are Driving Up House Prices* [online]. Available at www.confused.com/press/releases/2019/catchment-crisis [Accessed 14 November 2020].

Cotton, B., 2019, 'What Makes Birmingham the Perfect Business Destination?', *Business Leader* [online]. Available at www.businessleader.co.uk/what-makes-birmingham-the-perfect-business-destination/74288 [Accessed 14 November 2020].

Emoov, 2017, *Does Living Close to a Hospital Increase the Value of Your Home?* [online]. Available at www.emoov.co.uk/news/hospital-areas-perform-best-property-value [Accessed 14 November 2020].

'House prices in Hemel Hempstead', available at https://www.zoopla.co.uk/house-prices/browse/hemel-hempstead/?q=hemel%20hempstead [Accessed 28 May 2021]

The Independent, 2017, *Living Near This Shop Could Boost Your House Price by Thousands of Pounds*, 29 May 2017 [online]. Available at www.independent.co.uk/property/house-prices-latest-waitrose-effect-sainsburys-marks-and-spencer-uk-property-a7760926.html [Accessed 14 November 2020].

James, C., 2019, 'Property Prices Surges Near Football Stadiums in the UK', *ABC Money* [online]. Available at www.abcmoney.co.uk/2019/08/21/property-prices-surges-near-football-stadiums-in-the-uk/ [Accessed 14 November 2020].

Johns&Co, 2020, *How Does the Proximity to Supermarkets Affect House Prices in London?* [online]. Available at www.johnsand.co/proximity-to-supermar-kets-affect-house-prices-in-london [Accessed 14 November 2020].

Jones, R., 2017, 'How Much Is Living Near a Hospital Worth?', *Property Reporter* [online]. Available at www.propertyreporter.co.uk/property/ow-much-is-living-near-a-hospital-wor.html [Accessed 14 November 2020].

Jones, R., 2021, 'Government Introduces First Leasehold Reforms', *Financial Reporter* [online]. Available at www.financialreporter.co.uk/finance-news/government-introduces-first-leasehold-reforms.html [Accessed 10 January 2021].

Lee, T., 2018, 'How Stadium Investment Affects Property Prices in Surrounding Areas', *Pure Property Finance* [online]. Available at www.purecommercial finance.co.uk/news/how-stadium-investment-affects-property-prices-in-surrounding-areas/ [Accessed 14 November 2020].

McCord, J., McCord, M., McCluskey, W., Davis, P., McIlhatton, D., and Haran, M., 2014, 'Effect of Public Green Space on Residential Property Values in Belfast Metropolitan Area', *Journal of Financial Management of Property and Construction*, 19(2), pp. 117–137.

Ons.gov.uk, 2020, *UK House Price Index – Office for National Statistics* [online]. Available at www.ons.gov.uk/economy/inflationandpriceindices/bulletins/housepriceindex/january2020 [Accessed 14 November 2020].

Pettyson, 2020, 'House Prices: 13 Weird Things That Can Affect Your Property's Value', *Pettyson* [online]. Available at www.pettyson.co.uk/about-us/our-blog/271-affect-property-value [Accessed 14 November 2020].

Pollara, P., 2020, 'Could a Decent Local Pub Boost House Prices Near You?', *Mail Online* [online]. Available at www.dailymail.co.uk/property/article-8507483/Could-decent-local-pub-boost-house-prices-near-you.html [Accessed 14 November 2020].

Russell Group, 'Our Universities' [online]. Available at https://russellgroup.ac.uk/about/our-universities/#:~:text=In%202018%2D19%2C%20446%2C450%20undergraduates,at%20a%20Russell%20Group%20university [Accessed 7 May 2021].

Struttandparker.com, 2018, 'How New Transport Infrastructure Affects Property Prices and Saleability', *Strutt & Parker* [online]. Available at www.struttandparker.com/knowledge-and-research/how-new-transport-infrastructure-affects-property-prices-and-saleability [Accessed 14 November 2020].

What Mortgage, 2020, *Property Price Rises in University Cities Could Cover Tuition Fees* [online]. Available at www.whatmortgage.co.uk/news/buy-to-let/property-price-rises-university-cities-cover-tuition-fees/ [Accessed 14 November 2020].

Which, 2019, '16 Properties to Avoid If You Want to Get Mortgage', *Which?* [online]. Available at www.which.co.uk/news/2019/02/revealed-16-homes-to-avoid-if-you-want-to-get-a-mortgage/ [Accessed 14 November 2020].

Zoopla, 2021, *House Prices in Birmingham* [online]. Available at www.zoopla.co.uk/house-prices/birmingham [Accessed 21 March 2021].

Zoopla, 2021, 'House prices in North West England', available at https://www.zoopla.co.uk/house-prices/browse/north-west-england/?q=north%20west%20england. [Accessed 28 May 2021].

CHAPTER FIVE
NEGOTIATING THE PRICE OF YOUR PROPERTY

For many first-time buyers, negotiation is a source of great anxiety. This is not surprising because it is the first-time you have to do so and especially as you are making the biggest purchase ever in your lifetime. Your anxiety may arise from many factors, but the two key causes are: not being sure what the right price would be and not having experience in negotiation.

Negotiation is the process where you discuss with the seller with the aim of reaching a price that is acceptable to you both. Such an action is necessary because you and the seller have diverging interests. Naturally you want a lowest possible price, while the seller a highest possible price. You therefore need to find a point of compromise. However, while channelling all your energy to focus on price, both sides could easily lose the sight of their main objective which is to buy the house, for the buyer, and to sell the house, for the seller.

In this chapter, we offer a tool kit that is easy for you to remember and apply when negotiating for your deal.

If you conduct a quick search online or in academic textbooks, there are many theories on negotiation – from business negotiation, through political negotiation, to hostage release negotiation. Quite often the definition of negotiation is dissected into different concepts such as negotiation, bargaining and haggling, but all seek the same outcome: an agreement. And of course, the notions of win-win, win-lose or lose-lose as outcomes are easy enough to understand but often hard to determine.

You could think that you have concluded a great deal but then later end up kicking yourself because you realise that you have paid a higher price than you should. You could think that you have got a great discount from the advertised price, but then later discover that you would have to put in more money to sort out many problems with the house; or you could decide to abandon a deal but then later regret it.

Assuming you have found the right house after a considerable time of searching, and the price is more or less within your affordability, would you rather lose it just because you want the price to be reduced by £1,000? So, if everything else is equal, the objective of buying the house which you like and can afford must be more important than buying the house you like at a marginally cheaper price.

But of course, it is also equally important that while buying the house you like and can afford, you must ensure that you do not pay over the odds for it. If you pay more than the right price, then it is not the right deal for you. But what is the right price?

It is important first to differentiate between the right price and the affordable price. The right price is the right value of the house you are buying, and the affordable price is an indication of your affordability. You could afford to buy a more expensive house than the house you want to buy. (Please see more about affordability in Chapter 8.)

Generally, the economic theory of price based on supply and demand is still applicable. If there are many of the same type of houses in the same location, then the supply is high and vice versa. Equally, if there are many buyers who can afford to buy at a certain price level, then the demand is high. There are a number of factors at play that determine the price at which the house will be advertised. As a first-time buyer, you could fairly be confident that the natural supply and demand law always works, which means – in short – the market will adjust the price of a house to the right price range. When the seller wants to sell a house, they will get from the estate agent an estimate at which they can sell, and this price is based on an average price of similar properties in the same location.

To know whether the price is right, it is important to differentiate a few price concepts. The advertised price you would see on a website, a newspaper or an estate agent's window is the price at which the seller and the agent hope to sell, often referred to as the **asking price**. The price at which the buyer is willing to pay is the **bidding price**. Although there are occasions in which a buyer may be willing to bid at a price higher than the asking price in order to secure the purchase, such cases are not common – but they do happen.

Generally, the price at which the buyer and the seller agree to conclude a deal is found somewhere between the asking price (often the higher price) and the bidding price (often the lower price), but it is not unusual that a buyer ends up paying the asking price, or equally a seller ends up selling at the bidding price. What determines where the price ends up is the ability of both sides, the buyer and the seller, to negotiate. But for you, first-time buyers, there are a few tools that you could use to know what the right price is.

To find out the right price for the house or flat you want to buy, the first places are the advertised media (websites, local newspapers) or a visit to the agents of the local area where you want to buy.

If you are interested in a certain locality and know what type and size of the house you want to buy, you should keep looking at houses in and around that area – the more frequently the better. This exercise will develop the subconscious awareness of the right price level when you see the house or flat you want to buy, which will then help you determine if the asking price is more or less acceptable.

Another exercise is to check on zoopla.co.uk to see how much similar houses in the vicinity have recently been sold for. Although this website is very useful, it is important to pay attention to the date of the sale for each house. The price may look very low for a certain street because no houses there have been sold for a few years. Or you may see some big price discrepancies between very similar houses which were sold at different times. On zoopla.co.uk, you can probably find out the price of the very house you want to buy as well. This price, if dated back too long in the past, may not offer any useful price guidance, but the recent ones may give you a good point of reference – only for reference.

Unlike many other transactions where the negotiation is conducted between two parties, when you are buying a house, there are normally *three* parties involved in the deal: the seller (sometimes referred to as the vendor), the estate agent and yourself (the buyer).

It is obvious that the seller makes the ultimate decision at the other end of the deal; however, quite often, you have to conduct the negotiation via the estate agent who represents the seller. Therefore, it is useful to understand the role of each party in the transaction.

Negotiating with the estate agent

Although playing the intermediary role, the estate agent has a high stake in the deal. This is because the agent will only get paid if a deal is concluded. If there is no deal, the agent will not earn anything. And, in the UK, it is the seller who pays the estate agent, not the buyer. Therefore, despite the inevitability that the agent works for, and in the interest of, the seller, he or she can only make money if a deal is to be agreed and concluded.

Do not think that estate agents always work for sellers who pay the sale commissions. The agents only work for themselves and only have their own interest at heart. That means they can work for you, the buyer, as well. For that reason, establishing some credibility and rapport with the agent can be crucial to your success. Keep the agent engaged during the buying process. Even if you can meet and negotiate directly with the seller, it is still important to keep the agent in the loop – not only as a matter of courtesy, but also because they can be of great help to you.

An important rule most agents always keep very clear in front of their minds is that their commission is based on a percentage of the sale value. This means a reduction in the sale price – while certainly reducing the agent's fee income – may not be so detrimental to them. For example, assuming the commission is 1.5 per cent of the sale price, and the house is advertised at £300,000, if the deal were to be concluded at the advertised price, the agent would earn £4,500 (£300,000 × 1.5 per cent). However, if there were a discount, say £10,000, and the house were sold at £290,000, the agent fee would be reduced only by £150. Table 5.1 shows the calculation.

While a £10,000 reduction in the price is significant for both the buyer (positively) and the seller (negatively), for the agent, the difference in fee is only £150. Thus, quite often, the agent would be ready to negotiate with the seller on behalf of the buyer to achieve the deal. So, why not negotiate?

Another important fact that can be useful for your negotiation with the agent concerns the initial advertised price. When a seller wants to sell a house, the estate agent would conduct a valuation and propose a price which the agent thinks is achievable. This valuation is often a very subjective process based on the knowledge of the agent and their own ability to complete the deal.

Table 5.1 Commissions and fees

	Sale price	Commission (%)	Fee income
Advertised price	£300,000	1.5	£4,500
Discounted price	£290,000	1.5	£4,350
Difference	£10,000	1.5	£150

However, very often an agent may propose to the seller a higher price in order to compete with other agents. Agent A may propose to her seller a sale price of £300,000 because she thinks it is realistic and achievable. But she may lose the contract to Agent B who proposes a higher price, say £315,000 to the seller. Once Agent B has won over the contract, and the house is now on his book, he could later persuade the seller to reduce the price to a more realistic price which is lower. Normally, after the house has been advertised a while and cannot sell because of the higher price, the agent would suggest the seller to lower the price to a more realistic level – especially if he or she knows the urgency of the sale from the seller.

As a first-time buyer, not being in a chain and having evidence of your financial readiness for the purchase (i.e. a confirmed mortgage offer from a bank, or a decision-in-principle, and your deposit) would go a long way in establishing your credibility. Any estate agent would love to work for you for free!

To help with your negotiation with the estate agent, you may want to divide your questions into two different sets:

Questions to ask before and during the viewing of the property

- Who is the seller? The seller could be the person who owns the property, a trustee or a solicitor selling on behalf of a deceased's family members.
- What are their reasons for selling? Death, divorce, debt or relocation?
- What do the sellers want? A quick sale, or the best price, or sell and rent for a short while?
- Are they in a chain? Are they selling to buy another house? Is the sale of their house conditional upon their new purchase?
- How long has the property been on the market?
- How many viewings and offers has it had?

Asking these questions can help you establish the level of motivation of the seller and the urgency of the sale. You usually find a motivated buyer in the following circumstances:

- Selling a house to settle a divorce
- Following a death
- Selling the house to pay off a debt
- Relocation

Sellers facing these situations normally need to complete the sale as quickly as possible, and price may not be the most important criterion for them.

Questions to ask the estate agents after the viewing

- *Is there any flexibility with the asking price?* The worst answer you could get is 'No', but quite often an agent would say to you 'Just make an offer and we will discuss with the seller'.
- *Do you think the seller would accept my offer at £ . . . ?* Again, the worst answer you could get is 'Sorry, no' or 'I'm afraid that would be too low'. But most agents would not mind saying 'I don't think so, but I can try to speak to the seller and let you know'.
- *You know I am not in a chain and I have a mortgage offer and deposit ready. I really like this house and I appreciate the price the seller wants to get, but houses in the same condition in this neighbourhood have sold at this price [lower price]. Would you mind speaking to the seller to see if there is anything can be done?* Again, the worst answer may be: 'I'm afraid not. The seller is very firm on the price.'

Negotiating with the seller

Sometimes the term *vendor* is used to refer to the seller. The seller can be either a construction company (or the builder) or a private seller.

Negotiating with the builder

If you are buying a brand-new home in a new block of flat or a newly built house in a new estate, it is very likely that you are buying from a builder. With builders, there are often printed price lists of the properties, which give you the feeling that the price is fixed. However, in reality, builders, like any other sellers of any products, are very receptive to the supply and demand law of pricing. They could in fact be more flexible with the price than a private seller because there is no emotional attachment to the houses they sell. Besides, like any other business, they need to meet sales targets, or they need to complete the sales of one site to move on to another. So, there is always room for negotiation. You could treat the salesperson of the building company as an estate agent. His or her interest is also to make a successful sale early rather than waiting for uncertainty, and many of them could earn a commission-based salary like an estate agent. You could ask similar questions to negotiate as you would ask an estate agent (see earlier). Like estate agents, builders would prefer to deal with first-time buyers who can show evidence of financial readiness and not being in a chain. So, just ask the questions. The worst thing that could happen to you is they would say 'no, sorry'. If they are not flexible with the price and you still want to buy the house, then ask 'what can you do to motivate me to buy the house?'. Sometimes it may not be a price discount, but it could be a certain incentive for you to complete the purchase quickly, such as stamp duty paid, free wooden flooring or some white goods.

Negotiating with private sellers

The sellers you are more likely to come across are private sellers. More often than not, they are the ones who want to sell their own dwellings to move somewhere else. Sometimes, you have the opportunity to meet them, ask them questions or even negotiate directly with them, but you shouldn't be surprised that there are many who do not want to meet potential buyers for various personal reasons. If you don't meet them, there is not much you can do except working with the appointed estate agent. However, if you could meet and talk to the seller, it would be much more beneficial to you.

You may have done your due diligence on the house or flat you want to buy, and you may have got a lot of information from the estate agent, but it wouldn't do any harm to reconfirm with the seller the information you have gathered before if you have the chance to meet him or her, or them. What you need to keep in mind is that there is always some emotional value attached to the house or the flat by the seller. This means the owner may value the house more than it is really worth. Their emotional attachments can come from various sources ranging from the nice neighbourhood, through a specific feature of the house, to certain personal memories. Understanding this could give some room for you to negotiate the price. But be polite and respectful when you negotiate because the seller may have different values, beliefs and preferences from yours.

Like with the estate agent, or with anyone for that matter, it is important to show respect and try to establish some rapport with the seller. It will certainly help with your conversation if you get to meet and negotiate with them.

Questions to ask sellers

There are many questions you could ask the seller when viewing the house but try to ask them those questions in a friendly and conversational approach. Depending on individual circumstances, the range of questions may vary, but the following examples of questions may help you establish the accuracy of information gathered or select the best way to negotiate (e.g. what questions to ask).

- What makes you decide to sell the house?
- How long have you put the house on the market?
- Have you been busy with people viewing the house?
- How many offers have you got?
- Why did the previous buyer withdraw from the purchase?
- Have you found anything you want to buy?
- When are you hoping to complete the sale?
- How flexible are you with the moving date?

Besides these questions, there are other specific questions related to certain things or issues of the house that you could ask the seller. Information collected from these questions also helps you with your price negotiation later.

- How old are the double-glazed windows?
- How old is the boiler?
- What is the household insurance premium?

There is always the very important question that you must ask the seller which is the question why they want to sell the house. But rather than asking the straight question 'why do you want to sell the house?', you could try 'what makes you decide to sell the house?'. If you ask why, the seller may find a logical reason to reply which sometimes may not necessarily be the real reason, and the answer tends to be more subjective. Asking what makes them decide to sell would give you more opportunities to explore a little deeper into their motivation to sell. They can tell you more reasons and the answers tend to be more objective.

There are indeed many reasons why someone wants to sell their home, but finding the reason can tell you a lot about the urgency of the sale or the motivation level of the seller to sell – important information for your negotiation. For example, the seller who wants to sell the house to move abroad to take up a new job would not want to delay the sale for the sake of a few thousand pounds if they know the buyer is serious and has all the finance in place. A couple who are going through an acrimonious divorce may want to complete the deal sooner than waiting to gain a few thousand pounds on a sale.

Here we are not suggesting you take advantage of people's difficult or unpleasant situations, but you should not overlook the fact that you – with your financial readiness – could help give them the solutions they are looking for.

When it comes to the actual negotiating conversation, you could again ask the same questions as you would ask the estate agent above, if you feel you can do it. However, if you are not ready and do not want to negotiate directly with the seller, then just say thank you for the viewing and say you will be in touch with the agent.

Finally, the other important party in the deal is you.

Assuming you have done your due diligence about the house and are happy with your choice of home, how well prepared you are is an important factor in your ability to negotiate the price.

Suppose that we have two potential buyers, A and B, who both want to buy a house which is advertised for £250,000. A has a mortgage offer in principle and concrete evidence of deposit, and B has evidence of deposit money but no mortgage offer yet. Suppose that A asks for a £3,000 deduction in price and B is willing to pay the full asking price. Which buyer do you think would be the preferred candidate to the seller? A, of course. If the seller decides to go with B, they may run the risk that B might not get the mortgage offer and the deal would fall through. If they preferred the sureness of the sale, they should go with A. The amount £3,000 could be a lot of money for the seller, but the uncertainty of the sale with B could be even more costly.

Again, as a first-time buyer, your natural advantage is that you are not in a chain, which means, unlike non-first-time buyers, you do not have to sell anything to buy the house. But other than that, in order to negotiate you need to be financially ready for the purchase, that is, having a mortgage offer in principle and concrete evidence of deposit. Don't forget there are other buyers who also want to buy the house you like, too.

Another practical tip we would like to share with you, first-time buyers, that would help with negotiation is be yourself. Be yourself when you view the house, be yourself if you like something or not like something (subject to politeness, of course). Be honest with yourself that there are so many questions you want to ask about the house, its conditions and its neighbourhood. Feel free to express your concerns and anxieties and you may get the answers to them. Quite often, being open and frank with the seller will help establish a rapport. If everything else is equal, most sellers would prefer a buyer who appears to potentially fit in their own neighbourhood to one whom they do not personally like – even if they are moving out of the neighbourhood.

Your ability to negotiate depends very much on the information you get, so be frank and ask all the questions you want to ask. Be honest with yourself whether you are indeed buying what you really want or whether you have achieved your objectives which you have set out in terms of the house choice and the price. A couple of thousand pounds if spread out over 20 or 25 years of the mortgage may not be so significant. Price is important, but more crucial is the fact that you buy the house in which you can live happily. So, while negotiating for a price discount, be honest with yourself about whether you like the house. For you may achieve a good discount but may not like the house that much. In such a case, you may run the risk that you are negotiating with yourself!

Chapter Six
How to raise money for a deposit

Raising money for a deposit is seen by many as one of the main barriers to achieve the dream of owning a property, as UK lenders do not offer 100 per cent mortgages. Furthermore, the amount of deposit required is substantial because house prices have increased significantly. In October 2019, the typical first-time buyer deposit was 22 per cent of the purchase cost (around £48,543) or 172 per cent of an average salary (Money Charity, December 2019, p. 10). According to the Bank of England (BoE), around 75 per cent of renters are unable to buy a property due to a lack of sufficient savings to meet deposit requirements, rather than a lack of affordability as a result of low household income (HM Treasury, 2021).

The English Housing Survey (national survey commissioned by the Ministry of Housing, Communities and Local Government) reports that most first-time buyers (85 per cent) used their savings to fund their purchase in 2018–19, and this proportion increased from 76 per cent to 85 per cent between 2017–18 and 2018–19 (*English Housing Survey*, 2018–19). Some (34 per cent) received help from family or friends, and 6 per cent used an inheritance as a source of deposit.

Those who are successful in achieving their dream of home ownership are thought to be made up largely of high earners. In fact, 62 per cent of first-time buyers fall into the upper two income quintiles in 2018–19 – that is, households with annual incomes of more than £40,000. In addition, it is believed that first-time buyers from wealthier families are more likely to own their own home. The Santander First-Time Buyer Study in

2019 found that 43 per cent of young buyers surveyed have parents in a high occupational class (e.g. lawyers, accountants) (Santander, 2019, p. 17, *English Housing Survey*, p. 13).

Most people would probably agree that if you have a high income and wealthy parents, you have a higher chance of getting on the property ladder because it is easier, quicker and you have more choice in terms of lenders. However, do not feel despair if you do not belong to this category, as home ownership is still possible as there is a lot of help available. This chapter looks at the range of help available and what you can do to increase your chance of owning your own property.

Importance of planning

The first step you can take to increase your chance of climbing the property ladder is start to plan how you are going to achieve your goal. Planning is critical because it requires you to think about your future needs and take appropriate actions now to get there.

The process of planning to buy a property requires you to start thinking about two essential issues:

a) What is your approximate budget for your first property, as this determines how much you need to save?
b) What is your timeframe, as this affects how much you need to save per month?

Many first-time buyers appear to have an unwritten plan. The Santander First-Time Buyer Study in 2019 shows that many first-time buyers are aiming for an average deposit of nearly £25,000 (though the average is nearly £50,000). They plan to save over four years, which means an average saving of £6,200 a year or £517 per month. Many thus appear to know what they need to do to achieve their goal.

However, nearly a third have not taken steps to start saving, while others have taken a range of actions to reduce expenses and increase income (Santander, 2019). There is also a gender difference, with men able to save more than women (£11,660 saved compared to £5,620). The proportion of men who have not saved anything at all is also lower than that of women, 35 per cent in comparison to 48 per cent of women who have not saved anything. There may be a link between living at home and saving. A higher proportion of young men live with their parents than young women, and thus may be able to save more. In 2018, for example, over 31 per cent of men aged 20 to 34 years lived with their parents, compared to around 20 per cent for women (Office for National Statistics, Families and Households, 2019).

Three elements of planning

Goal setting

Although some first-time buyers may understand how much they need to save for a deposit, they may lack clear goals which weaken their motivation and discipline.

Goal setting is therefore a fundamental element of planning because it forces you to focus, organise and prioritise, as well as become more aware of your current financial situation and future needs.

To be successful, goals need to meet two essential conditions. Firstly, goals need to be SMART, an acronym for the following:

Specific: Goals need to be specific enough to suggest clear action. For example: 'I need to save money to pay for a deposit and upfront costs.'

Measurable: Successful goals are those that can be measured: 'I need to save £25,000 for a house deposit and £5,000 for costs.'

Attainable: Goals need to be reasonable: 'I need to save £500 per month over the next 60 months (five years).'

Realistic: Goals need to be realistic: 'I can save £500 per month by reducing my spending and getting a part-time job and working more hours.'

Time-related: Goals have a target date: 'Save £30,000 in five years by 1 July 2025.'

Once you set the goals, it is important that they are visual. Thus, rather than keep them in your head, goals need to be written down on a piece of paper and put somewhere where you can see them on a regular basis. This serves as a constant reminder, prompting you to take action and enhancing your motivation, determination and focus.

Living within your means

After setting goals, the next step is to organize your finances, if you have not done so already. It is important to avoid unnecessary borrowings, such as credit card debt, overdraft or unsecured loan, as an outstanding debt will reduce the amount you can borrow to buy a property. While borrowing allows you to spend more now, you will have less income to spend in the future because you need to use some of it to pay interest on the debt. Lenders therefore take debt into account and reduce the amount they are willing to lend.

The best way to avoid unnecessary debt is to ensure that you live within your means – that is, spend less than you earn. This is common sense but in practice many people find it difficult to do so, as can be seen in the high level of personal debt and a lack of savings in the UK. The best way to avoid over-spending is to budget your expenses and track spending. Budgeting can enable you to take control of your finances and shape your future because it involves thinking ahead and planning your expenditure in advance. It helps you avoid over-spending because budgeting requires you to set limits on each category of expenses.

According to Brian Tracy (a Canadian-American public speaker and self-development author), if you can drive a wedge between your earnings and the costs of your lifestyle, and save and invest the difference, you will become financially independent in your working lifetime (Tracy, 2020).

Brian Tracy therefore recommends two actions:

- Firstly, stop all non-essential expenses and draw up a budget of your fixed, unavoidable costs per month and aim to limit your expenditures temporarily to these amounts. Then, you carefully examine every expense and look for ways to economise or cut back. Aim for a minimum of a 10 per cent reduction in your living costs over the next three months.
- Secondly, learn to save and invest 50 per cent of any increase in your earnings from any source and commit to live on the rest. This still leaves you the other 50 per cent to do what you want, and do this for the rest of your career.

Save regularly

If you are planning to buy a property, you need to begin to start saving regularly. This is important because lenders and solicitors often require you to show that you have the money to pay for a deposit by providing three to six months' worth of bank statements. These are also used to satisfy money laundering requirements and show that your money comes from a legitimate source. Regular saving is also important because it introduces financial discipline and ensures that you live within your means.

Many people find it difficult to save because they do not prioritise saving. When they receive their salary, it is common to spend first and then save what is left over at the end of the month. This makes it difficult to save due to the invisible hand of Parkinson's Law. This stipulates that no matter how much money we earn, *there just isn't enough money* to cover our expenses, let alone pursue other goals, because our spending automatically adjusts to a new level of income. As we feel wealthier, we spend more. Our expenses rise as our earnings increase, leaving us no better off and we continue to live from payday to payday.

Financially smart individuals (e.g. Warren Buffet, one of the richest men in the world) therefore put aside a percentage of their income before they start spending money. This method, known as 'paying yourself first', is a powerful technique because it involves prioritizing saving over spending and forcing you to save.

Personal finance experts recommend that we should save at least 10–15 per cent of our income on a regular basis. They also advise to put savings in a separate bank account to reduce the temptation to spend and automate the process of saving by setting up a direct debit or standing order.

In summary, planning to buy a property requires you to plan your future, live frugally and tightly control your expenditure until you have saved enough for the deposit, and put away 10–15 per cent of your income for the future. You also need to organize your finances and become financially disciplined, so that whatever happens, you can meet your mortgage payments.

Three ways to save more quickly

You might want to save a large sum more quickly to enable you to climb the property ladder sooner. There are three steps you can take to increase the amount of money you can save.

Reduce expenses

The most popular method to save money is to reduce spending. More than half (57 per cent) of those interviewed by Santander First-Time Buyer Study plan to save money by cutting down on unnecessary spending (25 per cent), cutting back on socialising (20 per cent) and moving to a cheaper property/area (12 per cent).

As the cost of accommodation is normally the biggest expenditure, perhaps this should be the first area to review.

LIVE AT HOME

Moving back home to live with your parents/family may not be ideal, but it may enable you to achieve your goal sooner as you can save a lot of money. You might not need to pay rent, bills or even food. A couple in Wales were able to save £1,000 per month (£12,000 per year) by moving in with their parents temporarily (Hamilton, 2015).

In fact, moving back with parents is a popular strategy to save money. Between 1999 and 2019, the number of young people between 20 and 34 living at home rose by 46 per cent from 2.4 million to 3.5 million (Collinson, 2019). According to ONS, these figures mean that about one in four young adults now live with their parents (Office for National Statistics, 2019).

One of the key reasons why young adults stay at home is to save for the much higher deposit needed on their first home purchase. Georgie Laming of campaign group Generation Rent said:

> Young people are facing an impossible choice: either stay, if you're lucky, living in your childhood bedroom in the hope you can save a deposit – or rent and face a struggle to put money aside. Two thirds of private renters have no savings whatsoever.
>
> (Collinson, 2019)

Thus, short-term sacrifices can help you achieve your goal quicker.

Yet, only a small proportion (7 per cent) of those interviewed by Santander First-Time Buyer Study in 2019 sees moving in with a family member as an option. This suggests that moving back home may not be an option for some, as their job might be far away from home or their parents may not live in this country.

FIND CHEAPER ACCOMMODATION

If you cannot move back home, you can still save money by finding cheaper accommodation.

A higher proportion of young people see this as a more viable option to save money. According to Santander First-Time Buyer Study in 2019, a total of 12 per cent interviewed sought to save money, by moving to either a cheaper rental property or a cheaper rental area.

In addition, moving into a shared house is another way to save money. This is usually cheaper than renting alone, giving you the chance to save up for a place of your own.

Downsizing can also help you save money. Weigh up how many bedrooms you need and look for cheaper accommodation, perhaps closer to work, so that you can save money on commuting costs as well.

GET A LODGER

If you live alone and have the space, taking in a lodger can be a great way to help subsidise the cost of renting. You will be able to split the cost of your household bills as well as the rent. This gives you extra money to save for a deposit.

Before you begin your search for a new flatmate, check your landlord is happy for you to share your property and sub-let a room.

The easiest way to find a lodger you can trust is by asking friends, family, or asking your partner to move in. There are also plenty of websites (e.g. www.spareroom.co.uk) that allow you to advertise for free or for a small fee.

AWARE OF SMALL EXPENDITURE

Many of us tend to focus on big items of expenses and overlook small expenses. As Benjamin Franklin, one of the wealthiest men in the US, warned: 'Beware of little expenses; a small leak will sink a great ship.'

Small expenses can add up to a substantial amount. David Bach, in his book *Automatic Millionaire*, recommends us to be careful with expenditure on items such as money spent on drinks at Starbucks or Costa Coffee, bottled water, sandwiches or cigarettes, as these can add up and can prevent us from achieving our goals.

Increase income

A second popular method to increase savings is by earning more money. A high proportion of young people (44 per cent) interviewed by Santander First-Time Buyer Study in 2019 plan to save more by increasing income through working longer hours, starting a new job, pushing for a promotion and taking on an additional job.

A disadvantage of this method is that you are not in control of the process. Your employer decides whether you can work more hours or get promotion. If you are not successful with this, you are not able to save. Setting up your own business (e.g. selling on Amazon and eBay) gives you more control and it might be worthwhile to explore.

Convert unwanted items into cash

You can also raise money for the deposit by selling items which you no longer need, use or want, including clothes, books, jewellery, car, furniture, electronics and so on. Some 10 per cent of young people interviewed by Santander for its First-Time Buyer Study 2019 plan to save by selling possessions.

How to use mortgages to deal with the deposit problem

Raising the necessary deposit is a challenge for many first-time buyers, but there are four possible strategies you can adopt to address this problem.

Buy part of a property

You may find a shared ownership property a more affordable alternative. Shared ownership and shared equity schemes involve purchasing part of a property and renting the rest, and although you would not own 100 per cent of your property right away, you will have a foot on the property ladder.

You will still need a deposit to get a mortgage for a part buy property, but you would only need to borrow 25, 50 or 75 per cent of the property value.

For example, to get a 90 per cent mortgage on a 50 per cent share of a £150,000 property, you would only need to find a £7,500 deposit, rather than the £15,000 you would need to buy the whole property.

Buy in a cheaper area

One obvious way to deal with the problem of raising a deposit is to buy a property in a cheaper area. This requires a smaller deposit and less time in saving.

As can be seen below, if you intend to buy in London, the amount of deposit is £40,000 or more. However, if you buy in other areas, you will need only half the amount required to buy in London.

Table 6.1 Required deposit in different regions

Region	Average property price	Average target deposit
London	£463,283	£39,526
East of England	£318,491	£27,298
West Midlands	£196,571	£22,282
East Midlands	£190,171	£21,720
Yorkshire & Humber	£162,129	£20,746
North West	£159,471	£19,533

Source: Santander First-Time Buyer Study (2019, p. 11)

Apply for a high loan-to-value mortgage

A third way is to apply for a high loan-to-value mortgage. Lenders no longer offer 100 per cent mortgages, but 95 per cent LTV mortgages are available. This means that you can borrow 95 per cent of the value of the property and only need to raise 5 per cent deposit. For example, if the property value is £100,000, a 95 per cent mortgage allows you to borrow £95,000 and you only need to find £5,000 for the deposit.

In 2018, it was reported that there were more than 300 mortgages at 95 per cent LTV (up from 253 a year ago), and rates were competitive at an average 4.02 per cent – down from 6.39 per cent ten years ago (Halifax Intermediaries, 2018).

However, because of COVID-19 and the risk of falling house prices, many lenders have reduced the loan-to-value and only offer a maximum of 85–90 per cent. This means that you need to put down a bigger deposit (10–15 per cent instead of 5 per cent). However, in the March 2021 Budget the UK government announced the mortgage guarantee scheme for 95 per cent mortgages to encourage lenders to offer high loan-to-value mortgages during the pandemic. The government sees this intervention as temporary and believes that the number of high value mortgages will rise again once the economy returns to normal (HM Treasury, March 2021).

Although this reduces the need to raise a large amount of deposit, a high loan-to-value mortgage comes with several disadvantages, including paying more interest on the loan, facing the risk that the value of your mortgage might become higher than the value of your home (known as negative equity) and getting less favourable interest rates. However, it can help you get on the property ladder and you can move to a cheaper mortgage deal once the property appreciates in value.

Find a vendor gifted deposit

A fourth strategy is to look for deals that do not require you putting down your own money. While a deposit might be needed for a mortgage, this can come from the people selling the property, such as family, a builder or a private seller. This is known as a vendor gifted deposit.

Gifted deposit does not involve money changing hands, but only creating two prices: a gross price (the value of the property) and the net price (price agreed with the seller).

Some banks allow unlimited amount of deposit from family members (often parents). For example: imagine you buy a house from your family valued at £200,000 and you buy it for £100,000. The £100,000 difference or 50 per cent could be structured as vendor gifted deposit. However, you must state that the price of the property is £200,000 and the deposit £100,000.

Banks, however, only allow 5 per cent gifted deposit if you buy from a builder. Thus, if you buy a property for £200,000 from a builder, you are only allowed 5 per cent or £10,000 as a vendor paid deposit.

Some lenders accept vendor gifted deposit given by landlords. The Halifax, for example, accepts up to 10 per cent vendor gifted deposit from landlords. For example, the property is worth £200,000 and your landlord agrees to sell for £180,000, the difference of £20,000 (10 per cent) could be used as gifted deposit.

When using gifted deposit, it is important that you state the gross price in your mortgage application. For example, the house is worth £200,000 but the vendor agrees to sell the property at £190,000, giving you a 5 per cent gifted deposit. Instead of stating £190,000 as the house price on the application form, you state the gross price of £200,000 and put the £10,000 difference as gifted deposit. If you then apply for a 95 per cent mortgage, you do not need to worry about finding a 5 per cent deposit because in effect you receive 100 per cent finance.

Help from the government

The government recognizes that raising the deposit is a challenge. It is therefore offering help in two ways.

a) **Help to Buy: Equity Loan**: Under this scheme, the Government lends you up to 20 per cent of the cost of your newly built home, so you'll only need a 5 per cent cash deposit and a 75 per cent mortgage to make up the rest. You will not be charged loan fees on the 20 per cent loan for the first five years of owning your home. The disadvantage with this scheme is that it is only available on new build properties, which tend to be more expensive, and you still need to come up with a 5 per cent deposit. This will be discussed more in Chapter 7.

b) **Savings scheme**: The government also gives you an incentive to save by giving you a bonus. In 2017, the government introduced a Lifetime Individual Savings Account (LISA), a new type of Individual Savings Account to help you save for a home, retirement or both. The initiative was launched to try and combat the issue of those under 40 struggling to balance saving for retirement and a house deposit.

The key criteria are:

- You can open an account if you are between 18 and 39 years old (but you can contribute to age 50)
- The maximum you can save in a LISA is £4,000 per year
- You receive a government bonus of 25 per cent (i.e. £1,000 per year based on the maximum contribution, and the maximum total contribution is £5,000 per year)
- You can only use the money in a LISA account to buy your first property or fund retirement

As each year gives you a maximum bonus of £1,000, saving money for a longer period enables you to receive more bonus. The maximum number of years you can contribute is 32 years, giving the maximum amount of bonus of £32,000.

If the average amount of deposit required is £50,000, this will take about ten years, assuming that you save £4,000 per year (£333 per month), and the government adds £1,000 per year on top. This means saving 20 per cent of net income, assuming a salary of £28,000 per year (or net £1,881 per month).

Table 6.2 LISA: maximum bonus and maximum number of years of contribution

Maximum personal contribution per year	Max bonus per year	Total saving per year with bonus	Maximum amount of personal contributions over 32 years	Maximum number of years of contribution with bonus	Maximum bonus	Maximum amount saved with bonus over 32	Return on investment
£4,000	£1,000	£5,000	£128,000	32	£32,000	£160,000	25%

Table 6.3 How long does it take to build a deposit?

Amount of deposit required	£25,000	£50,000	£75,000	£100,000
Number of years based on maximum contribution per person	5	10	15	20
Number of years based on two people	2.5	5	7.5	10
Contribution per month	£333	£333	£333	£333

However, if you buy a property jointly with someone who also has a LISA, you can combine them, meaning that you get two sets of government bonus. If each of you saves the maximum per year, it might take five years to save, rather than ten years.

Help from parents: the Bank of Mum and Dad

Almost one in four first-time buyers now receive help from their parents, known as the 'Bank of Mum and Dad'. In 2019, Legal and General reported that parents gave their children £6.26 billion to help them get on the property ladder (Legal and General, 2019).

There are several ways parents could help their children.

Gifting money

The simplest method is gifting money. Family or friends can give all – or a portion – of a deposit to you as a simple, tax-free, non-returnable gift. This is the simplest option, allowing you to access the full range of mortgage options on the market.

Gifted money, however, could be subject to inheritance tax. For gifts above an annual allowance of £3,000, your parents must live longer than seven years from the date they gave you the money to avoid inheritance tax.

If your parents cannot afford to give a deposit away, they can lend you the money on their terms. A solicitor is needed to draw up the terms and, just like with a mortgage, the parents would register a charge on the property deeds to ensure the loan is paid back. The charge on the deeds would specify that on the sale of the property, or when it is remortgaged, the money lent is repaid.

Opening a savings account

Some specialist lenders offer a 100 per cent mortgage if this is tied to a savings account.

This allows first-time buyers to buy a house without a deposit on the condition that a family member deposits money in an attached savings account for a fixed period.

For example: Barclays Family Springboard and Lloyds Lend A Hand require 10 per cent of the value of the house to be locked away in a fixed-interest savings account for three years.

Although your money is tucked away and you cannot access it in an emergency, you will get it back, along with interest, when the term ends.

But for the first-time buyer, it may mean they have to stay in the property until its value increases enough to give them a substantial deposit in order to take the next step on the housing ladder.

If the house price falls, they could find themselves in negative equity. If mortgage payments are missed, banks may hold on to the money for longer until they are cleared, or, depending on the lender, use some of the money to clear any debts.

A major drawback of this method is that many family members or parents may not have the money or afford to have it tied up for a few years.

Setting up a family offset mortgage

Families can also use a savings account to reduce the interest a first-time buyer pays on their mortgage.

A family offset mortgage is similar to the savings and mortgage account option, but instead of getting interest on the money in the account, it is used to reduce the mortgage cost for a first-time buyer.

When the mortgage lender checks whether the first-time buyer can afford the mortgage, they will base the assessment on the lower monthly payments, after the parents' savings have been taken into account.

For example, if a mortgage of £150,000 was taken out, and £50,000 savings were deposited in the account, the borrower would only pay interest on £100,000 of the mortgage.

Parents will get their money back after a fixed period. The drawback is that the money is tied up for a period and will not earn interest for the parents. The value of the savings could also be reduced by inflation.

In addition, if the house is repossessed or sold for less than the amount borrowed, a lender can use the savings in the offset account to pay for the shortfall. The parents, therefore, have little control over their savings.

Putting a charge put on parents' home

Another option for families is, instead of offering cash as a deposit, parents can allow the bank to put a charge on their home for the equivalent amount, and this enables the child to apply for 100 per cent finance.

For example, a child buys a property worth £200,000 and needs a 10 per cent deposit (£20,000). A bank registers a charge of £20,000 on the parents' property. However, this might only be allowed if the parents' property has no mortgage, so that lenders can register a first charge on the property, rather than the second charge which puts them on a lower priority order of claim. In the early days, most of the mortgage repayments are used to reduce the amount charged on the parents' property.

This scheme is more complicated than the cash option because very few lenders offer this type of mortgage. In addition, parents may not qualify if they still have a mortgage on their own property. There is also the risk to their own property to consider in the event their child is not able to meet mortgage payments.

Cashing in on parents' or relatives' home

Parents or grandparents with a lot of equity in their homes can also help by releasing money through a scheme known as equity release. According to Canada Life, in the first half of 2018, close to 20 per cent of borrowers who took out equity release used the money to help family members.

Equity release is available to borrowers aged 55 or over and allows them to take money from their property now, rather than wait until they die or until the property is sold. When taking money out through equity release, the homeowner can defer both the payment of interest and capital until the property is sold when they die. However, the disadvantage with this is that interest is rolled up and added to the loan monthly, and this can double the debt every 14 years. The other option is to defer only the capital payment but pay monthly interest now.

Equity release is popular because homeowners can take money out and continue to live in their home. It is used by some families as a strategy to reduce inheritance tax liability, because the value of the equity release loan will be deducted from the overall estate before the inheritance tax bill is calculated. However, there are risks with this method and parents or grandparents should seek legal advice (Partington, 2019).

Help from employers

Saving for a deposit is one of the most serious financial challenges for young workers, especially in London. Some forward-thinking firms offer their staff help with getting on the housing ladder.

In 2016, it was reported that one company in London introduced a homebuyer perk. The company allows staff to deposit up to 20 per cent of their basic salary and all of their bonus into a special scheme.

At the end of three years, the company tops up the general savings by 50 per cent and the bonus savings by a third. When the employee buys a home, the money is transferred to the solicitor involved in the purchase (Hamilton, 2016).

It is unclear how many employers offer this kind of scheme. However, some employers might be able to offer interest-free loans, and it is, therefore, worthwhile to explore this with your employer.

Money pools

In some countries, you can borrow from people you know, through a system of **money pools**. A group of people contribute on a regular basis to a common fund and members take turns collecting the resulting lump sum. So, for example, ten people might contribute £100 each month to a money pool and take turns collecting £1,000 each over ten months.

Money pools are one of the world's oldest saving mechanisms, started over 1,000 years ago. They have many names – Fokontany in Madagascar, Hui in Taiwan, Pandero in Peru and Cundina in Mexico (Paypal, 2020). Money pools are also found in the UK, often in ethnic groups who have carried on the tradition from their original countries of origin.

Paypal launched *Money Pools* service in 16 countries in 2017 to allow people to borrow money through this method. In the UK, it appears that money pools are used for group travel, group gift or days out, but there is no reason why it cannot be used for other purposes.

Acquisition costs

Besides the need to raise a deposit, you will also need to find money to pay for acquisition costs, such as valuation fees, legal costs and stamp duty. These fees are paid to the lender, solicitor and government, respectively.

Lender's fees

There are a few fees payable to the lender, as outlined in Table 6.4.

A valuation of a property is compulsory before a mortgage can be approved. There are three types of valuation: a basic valuation, a Home Buyer Report and a structural survey. While a basic valuation is carried out to ensure that the property is a suitable security for the loan, a Home Buyer Report is more detailed and documents any problems in a property that could cause damage and need future repairs. A structural survey is recommended for older properties or those that are built from non-standard materials. It is the most expensive survey because surveyors can be sued if they fail to report any structural problems which might surface later.

Lenders can offer a free valuation but this is restricted to a basic valuation report. If you would like to have a more detailed report before buying, you need to pay for this cost upfront.

However, a popular incentive given by lenders is cashback, a sum payable to borrowers on completion, and this can be used for any purpose.

In addition, lenders allow some fees to be added to the loan, so that you can pay over a period of time. One disadvantage of doing this is that you will have to pay interest on the fees.

Legal fees

In addition to lender's fees, there are also legal costs involved, as listed in Table 6.5.

Some fees are VATable and so you have to pay 20 per cent more. Lenders can also offer free legal fees, but this is restricted to the solicitor's fee, not other costs (e.g. searches).

Table 6.4 Types of fees to lenders

Types of fees to lender	Description of fee	Amount	Upfront or added to loan
Valuation fee	Surveyor to provide an assessment of the property.	Cost depends on type of survey	Upfront
Booking fee			Can be added to the loan
Arrangement fee		Fixed amount or % of loan	Upfront or add to the loan

Table 6.5 Legal fees

Type of legal costs	Description of fee
Solicitor fee	Fee to carry out conveyancing work
Review mortgage offer	Fee to review mortgage offer
Land Registry and Land Charge Search fee	Fee to carry out land registry and land charge search
Land Registry fee	Fee to add ownership details on HM Land Registry
Local, Chancel, Environment and Water Search	Fee to carry out searches to check any local plans and problems
Completion of Stamp Duty Land Tax return	Fee to complete a stamp duty land tax return
Electronic Identity Search (per name)	Fee to carry out an identity search
Bank transfer fee (per transfer)	Fee to transfer money by bank transfer

The legal fee is higher for leasehold properties.

Fee to the government – stamp duty

Stamp duty is one of the biggest expenses in property purchase and it is paid to the government (via your solicitor) on the day you complete your purchase.

In England and Northern Ireland, you have to pay stamp duty when you buy a residential property, or a piece of land, costing more than £125,000 (or more than £40,000 for second homes). This tax applies to both freehold and leasehold properties, and buying outright or with a mortgage. The stamp duty rates in England and Northern Ireland are shown in Table 6.6.

From 22 November 2017, the government announced that first-time buyers buying a residential property for £300,000 or less in England and Northern Ireland would not have to pay Stamp Duty Land Tax (SDLT). If the price was between £300,000 and £500,000, they would only pay stamp duty on the amount in excess of £300,000. However, those purchasing a property for more than £500,000 would not be entitled to any relief and would pay SDLT at the normal rates.

In July 2020, the government announced that the stamp duty exemption threshold was to be increased to £500,000 until March 2021, and so first-time buyers would not pay any stamp duty if the price falls below this amount. The deadline has been extended till the end of June 2021.

Table 6.6 Stamp duty

Minimum property purchase price	Maximum property purchase price	Stamp duty rate
£0	£125,000	0%
£125,001	£250,000	2%
£250,001	£925,000	5%
£925,001	£1.5 million	10%
Over £1.5 million		12%

Source: Money Advice Service, 'Stamp duty'

The rates and thresholds are different in Wales and Scotland. In Scotland, you will pay Land and Buildings Transaction Tax (LBTT) for properties over £145,000 or £175,000 for first-time buyers. In Wales, buyers have to pay Land Transaction Tax (LTT) for properties over £180,000, and there are no exemptions or discounts for first-time buyers. The stamp duty nil rate band was increased to £250,000 until March 2021 in Scotland and Wales. The government also introduced a new rule from April 2016 which requires buyers of additional residential properties, such as second homes and buy-to-let properties, to pay an extra 3 per cent in stamp duty on top of current rates for each band in England and Northern Ireland. The surcharge is 4 per cent in Wales and Scotland.

Ongoing costs

Besides upfront costs, you need to be beware of the ongoing costs, such as insurance, council tax and utility bills.

The key difference between buying and renting lies in the ongoing costs commitments. When you rent, your rent may include all ongoing costs, but when you own your own place, it is your responsibility to pay mortgage and running costs. Therefore, buying involves a bigger financial commitment because ongoing costs, such as repairs, can be open-ended.

If you buy a flat, there might be additional costs such as leaseholder's costs and service charge. It is worthwhile to pay attention to service charge. This is a charge levied by a management company to carry out repairs and essential maintenance to the building. This charge can be large and crippling, and you have no control over this cost. For example, a few years ago, a client of mine ran into trouble. She owned an ex-council flat in London and the management company wanted to replace all windows in the building. She was given a bill of £8,000. When she

Table 6.7 Ongoing costs

Ongoing costs	Description	Insurance
Insurance	Insurance cover for your property and contents	
Council tax	Council tax to local government for services	
Running costs	Running costs include utility bills, water, gas	
Leaseholder's costs	Ground rent and service charge. Insurance is normally included in cost of service charge	
Maintenance and repairs	These include boiler breakdown, blockages, water leak, appliances breakdown	Can get insurance to avoid major outlays or setting up an emergency fund

could not pay, she was taken to court. Some people therefore prefer to buy a house as there is no service charge. However, in some areas, buyers might not have the option.

Summary

Having looked at ways to raise finance, the next chapter will examine in detail different government's schemes to help buyers get on the property ladder.

References

Bach, D., 2008, *The Automatic Millionaire Homeowner*. New York: Broadway Books.

Collinson, P., 2019, 'Record Numbers of Young Adults in UK Living with Parents', *The Guardian*, 15 November 2019 [online]. Available at www.theguardian.com/uk-news/2019/nov/15/record-numbers-of-young-adults-in-uk-living-with-parents [Accessed 14 November 2020].

English Housing Survey Headline Report, 2018–19 [online]. Available at https://assets.publishing.service.gov.uk/government/uploads/system/uploads/attachment_data/file/860076/2018-19_EHS_Headline_Report.pdf [Accessed 14 November 2020].

Halifax Intermediaries, 2018, 'First-Time Buyers – The New Generation', *Mortgage Solutions* [online]. Available at www.mortgagesolutions.co.uk/hub-page/2018/05/15/first-time-buyers-new-generation/ [Accessed 14 November 2020].

Hamilton, S., 2015, 'Your Eight Step Guide to Climbing onto the Property Ladder', *This Is Money*, 23 May 2015 [online]. Available at www.thisismoney. co.uk/money/mortgageshome/article-3094020/Living-parents-helped-raise-deposit-eight-steps-property-ladder.html [Accessed 14 November 2020].

Hamilton, S., 2016, 'Work Perks That Can Help You Buy a Home, Invest and Get Life Insurance', *This Is Money*, 6 February 2016 [online]. Available at www.thisismoney.co.uk/money/news/article-3435026/My-office-savings-scheme-enabled-buy-house-make-work-s-perks-life-insurance-help-home buying-job-gives-just-salary.html [Accessed 14 November 2020].

HM Treasury, 2021, *The Mortgage Guarantee Scheme: An Outline* [online]. Available at https://assets.publishing.service.gov.uk/government/uploads/system/uploads/attachment_data/file/965665/210301_Budget_Supplementary_Doc_-_mortgage_guarantee_scheme.pdf [Accessed 6 March 2021].

Legal and General, 2020, *Bank of Mum and Dad* [online]. Available at www. legalandgeneral.com/bank-of-mum-and-dad/bomad-report-2019.pdf [Accessed 14 November 2020].

Money Advice Service, *Stamp Duty – Everything You Need to Know* [online]. Available at https://www.moneyadviceservice.org.uk/en/articles/everything-you-need-to-know-about-stamp-duty#stamp-duty-on-second-homes [Accessed 7 May 2021].

The Money Charity, 2019, *Money Statistics* [online]. Available at https:// themoneycharity.org.uk/media/December-2019-Money-Statistics.pdf [Accessed 14 November 2020].

Office for National Statistics, 2019, *Families and Households in the UK* [online]. Available at www.ons.gov.uk/peoplepopulationandcommunity/births deathsandmarriages/families/bulletins/familiesandhouseholds/2018 [Accessed 14 November 2020].

Partington, S., 2019, 'Seven Ways to Get Help Your Child Buy Their First Home', *This Is Money*, 5 March 2019 [online]. Available at www.thisismoney.co.uk/ money/mortgageshome/article-6774663/Seven-ways-child-home-New-ways-help-kids-property-ladder.html [Accessed 14 November 2020].

Paypal, 2020, *Chip in for Group Gifts with Money Pools* [online]. Available at www.paypal.com/uk/webapps/mpp/money-pools [Accessed 16 November 2020].

Santander.co.uk, 2019, *Santander First-Time Buyer Study: The Future of the Homeownership Dream* [online]. Available at www.santander.co.uk/assets/ s3fs-public/documents/santander-first-time-buyer-study.pdf [Accessed 14 November 2020].

Tracy, B., 2020, 'Parkinson's Law', *Briantracy.com* [online]. Available at www. briantracy.com/blog/financial-success/parkinsons-law/#:~:text=Slow%20Down%20Your%20Spending&text=I%20call%20it%20the%20%E2%80%9Cwedge, as%20you%20make%20more%20money [Accessed 14 November 2020].

Chapter Seven
Government schemes to help first-time buyers

Between 2003 and 2014, the proportion of young people between 25 and 34 years old owning their own property decreased by 23 per cent (fell from 59 to 36 per cent), while the proportion living in private rented sector more than doubled (increased from 21 to 48 per cent).

By 2019, the trends appear to have been slightly reversed, as home ownership among the 25–34 years old rose by 5 per cent (from 36 to 41 per cent), and the proportion in private renting fell by 7 per cent (48 to 41 per cent) (*English Housing Survey Headline Report 2018–19*). Government initiatives introduced in this period may have helped young people get on the property ladder. The HM Treasury reports that the government assisted 681,000 households to purchase a home since 2010 through Help to Buy and Right to Buy, while the Help to Buy Mortgage Scheme helped 100,000 households (HM Treasury, 2021).

The government feels that it is necessary to help young people get on the property ladder because it is aware that many are frustrated for not being able to achieve their dream of home ownership. Their votes count, as young people (18–39 years old) form a significant proportion of the voters, making up more than 26 per cent of the population (Statista, 2020). By assisting young people to own their property, the government hopes to get their votes.

In addition, housing is a real source of wealth inequality in the UK. High levels of wealth inequality affect future social outcomes (e.g. social mobility), as property wealth is likely to cascade down the generations. Indeed, a report on home ownership and social mobility shows that the ability of young people to get on the housing ladder is now determined much more by whether their parents own their own home or not (Blanden and Machin, 2017; Cosslett, 2017).

High levels of wealth inequality are undesirable because it is believed that they cause a bias in the democratic process. In the US, Martin Gilens talks about the economic domination of the elite, and similar concerns of unequal influence of the wealthy have also been raised in the UK (Tilford, 2020).

One solution to help the poor while increasing political popularity at the same time is to adopt a policy known as asset-based welfare policy. Many people in the UK like to own a property, and so subsiding home ownership will enable low-income renters to buy their own homes. This has a positive effect because those who own an asset are believed to behave more responsibly as they have a stake in society.

This chapter examines measures adopted by the government to help first-time buyers in the UK in the last ten years and assesses the effectiveness of these.

Government schemes to promote home ownership in the UK

The UK government has been helping prospective buyers get on the property ladder through a number of schemes (Wilson et al., 2021). In the past, Shared Ownership and Right to Buy Schemes, offering buyers a huge discount, have played a key role in promoting home ownership, but these schemes are now not generally available to single, young people due to housing shortage and long waiting lists. Since 2013, the government has been focusing on measures such as interest-free loans, bonus for savings and stamp duty exemption. This chapter will examine these schemes in turn.

Right to buy

Many people in the UK have been able to climb the property ladder, thanks to the Right to Buy Scheme. When Margaret Thatcher came to power in 1979, local councils were big landlords, owning around 32 per cent of all dwellings in Britain, totalling some 6.5 million properties (Disney and Luo, 2020). However, council houses were costly to maintain and were an economic burden to local councils.

The Thatcher government therefore began to sell off council houses to reduce the burden and also to raise cash for local councils. The Housing Act of 1980 gave a statutory right for council tenants who had lived in their council house for three years to buy at a significant discount, varying from 33 per cent to a maximum of 50 per cent for those with 20 years' residence.

When the Labour Party came to power in 1997, they tightened the rules for selling council houses by reducing discounts. The Right to Buy discount was drastically reduced from £50,000 to a maximum of £16,000 (£38,000 for London).

In 2010, when the Coalition government came to power (Conservative and Liberal), they decided to reinvigorate the Right to Buy policy by increasing discounts. In April 2012, the maximum cash discount available for Right to Buy sales was increased to £75,000 across England, but those living in London were entitled to £100,000. From July 2014, the maximum cash discount available for the Right to Buy began to rise in line with the Consumer Price Index (CPI) rate of inflation. From April 2021, the discount is £112,800 for London and £84,600 for the rest of England (Gov. UK, 2021).

Overall, the Right to Buy Scheme contributed to the increase in home ownership from 55 per cent in 1979 to over 70 per cent in the early 2000s (Disney and Luo, 2020). Between 1979 and 2017, more than 4.5 million council properties had been sold, resulting in a reduction of local council housing to 2 million homes (Kentish, 2017). The Right to Buy has been successful in inducing a large-scale change in asset ownership among UK households.

Unfortunately, young people find it hard now to get on the property ladder through the Right to Buy Scheme due to the local council's allocation system. Council housing is normally allocated to families by a simple queuing mechanism with priority given to families with special housing needs (state of existing accommodation, severe health problems, eviction unrelated to personal behaviour, homelessness, etc.) and to those with low incomes.

Getting a council house now is exceptionally difficult due to a lack of available social housing across the UK. As a result, there is a long waiting list. On 1 April 2018, there were 1.11 million households on local authority waiting lists. However, compared with 2017 when there were 1.16 million households, there were now 50,000 fewer households on the waiting list (Local Authority Housing Statistics, 2018).

For those without priority needs, waiting times could be as long as several years to an indefinite period. In 2017, the wait for a council property was more than ten years in some parts of the country (Kentish, 2017). It was reported that, in 2016, people in Barking and Dagenham, a deprived east London borough, had to face a 50-year wait for a council house. Barking and Dagenham, where the average property then cost £270,000, has seen almost 20,000 of its homes sold since the right-to-buy policy was introduced 1980, about half its total housing stock. It had 50 times more people on the housing waiting list than properties available (Walker, 2016).

In other parts of the UK, the situation is not better. In Birmingham, there are reports of up to 3,000 people at a time bidding on a single property in 2020. As a result, some families have ended up homeless and being housed in Bed & Breakfast accommodation and temporary shelter. Some people are believed to have been applying for a council house for the past 13 years, while another had placed more than 650 bids but not received a single offer (Chamberlain, 2020).

The Right to Buy Scheme has been blamed for causing the shortage of affordable housing. Many of the flats that first-time buyers are able to afford have now been sold off and are being rented out privately – indeed, over 40 per cent of properties purchased under the RTB scheme are now being rented out. The average private rent in England is much higher than social rent (Kentish, 2017). It appears that the Right to Buy Scheme has discriminated against young and single people who do not receive priority in the allocation queue.

Shared ownership

A less popular method of climbing the property ladder is the Shared Ownership Schemes, an initiative which was launched in the late 1970s. Shared ownership allows a housing association or a local council tenant to purchase a share of a home (between 25 and 75 per cent) and pay rent on the part they do not own. Tenants will then be given the chance to buy further chunks of the home as and when they can afford it, under what is known as 'staircasing' until they own 100 per cent.

To qualify for the Shared Ownership Scheme, tenants must be a first-time buyer and that their household income must not exceed £80,000, or £90,000 in London. The scheme is available on both new-build and resale properties.

On sale, owners only make a profit on the portion of the property they own. The remainder will go to the housing association or council. If there is a loss, this will also be split between the owner and the council or housing association relative to the shares they own.

However, the Shared Ownership Scheme is very competitive as there is more demand than supply. It is difficult to buy a property through this scheme for two reasons. Firstly, affordable housing gives priority to people from certain occupational backgrounds, such as nurses, firefighters, other key workers and army personnel. Certain tenants, such as housing association and council tenants, and families and couples also get priority, while single people do not (Bieoley, 2018).

Secondly, it is difficult to get a mortgage. Research carried out by the Cambridge Centre for Housing and Planning Research (May 2012) found that out of 145,000 shared ownership purchases in England since 2001, only 27,908 (over 19 per cent) had stair-cased up to full ownership. Factors which prevent many people from gaining full ownership include high transaction costs, unavailability of mortgage finance and incomes failing to keep pace with house prices (Wilson et al., 2017).

Interest-free loans for a deposit

In 2013, the government introduced interest-free loans to help pay for a deposit under the Help to Buy Scheme. This contained two elements: Equity Loan and Mortgage Guarantee. However, the Mortgage Guarantee, where the government offered a guarantee to mortgage lenders to encourage larger loans, was scrapped at the end of 2016.

The Help to Buy Equity Loan requires a prospective buyer to put down a minimum 5 per cent deposit of the property value, with the government offering an interest-free loan of a further 20 per cent. The remaining 75 per cent is covered by a standard mortgage.

For example, on a £200,000 property, you would need a minimum deposit of £10,000 (5 per cent) and the means to qualify for a mortgage of £150,000 (75 per cent). The government would then provide an equity loan of £40,000 (20 per cent).

Help to Buy mortgages are offered by most major lenders including Santander, Barclays and Halifax, as well as some smaller building societies such as Teachers and Newbury.

How the equity loan works

- The Help to Buy Equity Loan scheme is only available on new-build properties in England and, there are regional differences in the maximum purchase price (e.g. London £600,000 while North East £186,100).
- There is no interest to pay for the first five years.

- In year 6, interest (known as a 'loan fee') kicks in at 1.75 per cent.
- It can only be used to buy your main residence and cannot be used to buy a second home or a buy-to-let property.

The idea with the Help to Buy Equity Loan is that, because you are theoretically only borrowing 75 per cent from the mortgage lender, interest rates will be cheaper than on a standard 95 per cent mortgage.

By January 2019, it was reported that more than 400,000 first-time buyers have used the scheme. The Help to Buy Equity Loan Scheme was closed to new applications in December 2020, and buyers were given until 31 March 2021 to complete their purchase. However, due to delays caused by the pandemic, the deadline was extended till 31 May 2021.

In other parts of the UK, the Help to Buy scheme is also available:

- Help to Buy (Wales) offers a government equity loan worth up to 20 per cent. It applies to new-build properties up to a maximum value of £300,000.
- Scotland's Help to Buy, known as the Affordable New Build Scheme, offers a government equity loan worth up to 15 per cent which always remains interest-free. The scheme applies to new-build properties up to a maximum value of £200,000.
- There is no Help to Buy scheme in Northern Ireland.

The government has confirmed that a new Help to Buy scheme will launch in England when the current scheme closes, and will run for two years until March 2023. However, this will be limited to first-time buyers only and price caps will be regional. The Help to Buy Scheme has also been extended in Wales and Scotland.[1]

Criticisms of Help to Buy Scheme

Benefit developers

The Help to Buy Scheme has been criticised as a 'terrible deal' as it is believed that the scheme has benefited developers more than first-time buyers for two reasons (Lawrence, 2019).

One of the requirements of the Help to Buy Equity Loans is that it can only be used to buy a new build property. While a new build property comes with advantages such as ten-year warranties, built with modern materials and to modern specs, many believe that you have to pay a 'new build premium'. The price of new-build properties is thought to be 16 per cent higher than comparable properties in the area in England and Wales. And just as a new car loses its value when it is driven out of a garage, a new-build property also loses value once it is lived in. The average new-build loses around half its premium when it is sold for the first-time.

Another requirement of the scheme is that the property must be bought from 'a registered Help to Buy builder'. This adds another premium onto the price that the first-time buyers are paying. A report by Morgan Stanley found that builders could charge an extra 5 per cent for the properties sold through the scheme. The combined effects of the new-build premium and the Help to Buy premium mean that people buying through Help to Buy are paying 21 per cent over the odds (Lawrence, 2019). In November 2019, the average price of a new-build property was £296,789, 20 per cent more than a second-hand property with an average price of £245,651 (UK House Price Index for January 2020).

Benefit high earners

Help to Buy London is an extension of the Help to Buy Equity Loan. It is aimed at people with a 5 per cent deposit who want to buy in London and Greater London, where house prices are typically much higher than the UK average.

Help to Buy London offers an equity loan of up to 40 per cent, compared to 20 per cent in England and Wales and 15 per cent in Scotland. The loan is interest-free for the first five years and, again, the scheme is available only on qualifying new-build homes.

This scheme is also being criticised because it is argued that high earners benefit more. About 4,000 help-to-buy loans issued in 2016 were handed to those earning £100,000 or more (Cosslett, 2017).

Benefit only a few

The Help to Buy Scheme has been criticised because it is believed that only a small number of people have benefited. In the seven years since the launch of the Help to Buy Equity Loan scheme from April 2013 to 31 March 2020, approximately 272,852 property purchases had been supported by the Scheme. First-time buyers accounted for 82 per cent of total home purchases using Help to Buy Equity Loan (224,133 properties).

Table 7.1 Bank of Mum and Dad

Year	2016	2017	2018	2019	Total
Number of properties supported	305,900	298,300	316,600	259,400	1,180,200
Value of properties (billions)	£77.49	£75.38	£81.71	£69.51	£304.09 billions
Value of lending (billions)	£5.37	£6.46	£5.71	£6.26	£23.8 billions

Source: Legal and General, *Bank of Mum and Dad* (2019, p. 3)

The equity loans have cost the government a total of £16.05 billion and have supported the purchase of £73.28 billion worth of property. This gives the value of individual loan at £58,639 and the average price £293,195 (Help to Buy Equity Loan Scheme, 2020).

The number of buyers assisted by Help to Buy Equity Loan is lower than that assisted by the Bank of Mum and Dad. In total, according to Legal and General, parents in the UK have assisted 1.18 million property purchases, 4.3 times higher than the number of purchases through Equity Loan Scheme.

In addition, Legal and General argues that Help to Buy is a minority funding stream because 61 per cent of first-time buyers say that they would not use schemes such as Help to Buy with their home purchase. Help to Buy also faces an uncertain future after its cut-off point in 2023 (extended from 2021). The Bank of Mum and Dad, by contrast, is entirely mainstream and is likely to stay for good.

However, the construction industry is important to the UK economy, contributing £117 billion (6 per cent of GDP) and creating 2.4 million jobs (Rhodes, 2019). The Help to Buy Equity Loan scheme is also designed to support this sector.

Bonus for savings

Help to buy ISA

The government also seeks to help first-time buyers to buy a property by giving them a 25 per cent bonus when they save. In 2015, the government introduced Help to Buy ISA to help young people save for a deposit. However, this scheme has several limitations.

1   The bonus was capped at £3,000 per buyer. Thus, to receive the maximum bonus, individuals needed to save £12,000, giving them a

total of £15,000 towards the deposit of their first property. This was well below the amount needed.

2 Although intended to help first-time buyers purchase their first home, the Help to Buy ISA bonus could not be put towards the initial deposit payable at exchange. Instead, the tax-free lump sum was paid directly to the mortgage lender at completion.

3 The Help to Buy ISA could only be used when the property price was less than £250,000 and £450,000 in London.

4 A Help to Buy ISA was a cash ISA and you could not invest in stocks and shares. This means that it was difficult to grow the money saved. You were also only permitted to pay into one cash ISA in each tax year.

Help to Buy ISA was closed to new applicants on Saturday 30 November 2019 (HM Treasury, *Help to Buy ISA*).

Lifetime ISA (LISA)

The Help to Buy ISA was replaced with Lifetime ISA in 2017. Again, this gives savers 25 per cent bonus and can only be opened by those between the age of 18 and 39 (though they can contribute up to the age of 50).

In many ways, a LISA is better than a Help to Buy ISA due to the following:

1 **Higher bonus**: An individual can contribute up to 32 years, giving them a total bonus of £32,000. This encourages long-term saving.

2 **Annual limit**: Maximum contribution per year is £4,000 and with £1,000 bonus, the saver will accumulate a maximum of £5,000 per year. However, this annual limit restricts the amount of bonus you can receive if you need to buy a house quickly.

3 **Higher property limit**: Savers can only use the fund in their Lifetime ISA to buy a property worth up to £450,000 anywhere in the UK. However, this means that those who buy in London might not be able to use their funds if the property price exceeds this threshold.

4 **Use for a deposit**: Savers can use their LISA funds to pay for the deposit.

5 **Investment options**: LISA can be invested in stocks and shares, and so there is potential to increase the value.

6 **Greater flexibility**: LISA can be used to buy a property or to fund retirement. This shows that the government recognises that young people under the age of 40 are struggling to save for a house and retirement.

By 2019, 223,000 LISAs had been taken out, worth £604 million (HM Revenue and Customs, *Individual Savings Accounts Statistics*, 2020, p. 21). However, LISA funds can only be used towards a property purchase after 12 months of opening an account, suggesting that one key aim is to encourage young people to get into the habit of saving.

Stamp duty

One of the most simple and direct ways to help first-time buyers is exemption from stamp duty. Stamp duty is payable on all residential properties over £125,000 in England and Northern Ireland. However, in November 2017, the government introduced a stamp duty exemption for first-time buyers (those who have never owned or part-owned a home previously anywhere in the world) who buy a property worth £300,000 or less. If the price is higher than this amount but less than £500,000, they pay the stamp duty on the difference between £300,000 and £500,000. If the property is more than £500,000, they are not entitled to any exemption.

For example, if a property costs £300,000, first-time buyers pay zero stamp duty as they get full exemption. If it costs £500,000, there is a 5 per cent stamp duty between £300,000 and £500,000 and so the stamp duty bill will be £10,000, opposed to the previous £15,000. The maximum saving available is therefore £5,000 (Zoopla, 2020).

Because of the adverse effects of COVID-19 on the housing market, the government increased the limit to £500,000 in July 2020 in an effort to stimulate the housing market in England and Northern Ireland. This scheme was originally set to end on 31 March 2021 and is estimated to cost £1.3 billion (Green, 2020). However, the stamp duty holiday has now been extended till September 2021.

Other proposals

Starter Homes scheme

Starter Homes were designed for first-time buyers aged between 23 and 40, offering them a minimum discount of 20 per cent of the market price with price caps set for £250,000, or £450,000 in London.

The scheme was first announced in 2015 with the first completions earmarked for 2018. The November 2015 Spending Review provided £2.3 billion to support the delivery of 60,000 Starter Homes (of the 200,000 previously announced).

However, an investigation by the National Audit Office found that the government had failed to deliver any of the 200,000 homes promised under the Starter Homes Initiative (Home Owners Alliance, 2019).

First Homes Scheme

The government is currently considering a proposal, known as First Homes Scheme. This scheme would allow first-time buyers to purchase a property in their local area for an average of nearly £100,000 below the market value.

However, the government has not confirmed how many of these homes it hopes to build, who will build them, or outlined any areas where the scheme could be trialled (Maunder, 2020).

What other measures could help first-time buyers to get on the property ladder?

Despite the initiatives introduced in recent years, the Santander First-time Buyer Study 2019 shows that three-quarters of would-be first-time buyers say that the government needs to do more to help them. The measures supported by aspiring first-time buyers include:

- Extend the Help to Buy scheme beyond 2023
- Cap rent prices
- Cut stamp duty for all house buyers on homes below £500,000 (to free up homes for first-time buyers)
- Encourage landlords to sell properties to their tenants by giving them tax incentives
- Stronger quotas on developers to build more affordable homes
- Increase the number of shared ownership properties available

The Santander First-Time Buyer Study proposes several measures to address the challenges facing first-time buyers:

1 **Deposits**: More should be done to help first-time buyers raise money for a deposit. For example: the Forces Help to Buy Scheme (allowing

those working in armed forces to take an interest free loan of up to 50 per cent of their salary towards a house purchase) could be extended to support all public sector workers.

Another potential solution could be a government-backed guarantee to lenders, reducing or removing the need for certain categories of first-time buyers to provide a deposit.

2 **Affordability**: Since 2008, lending criteria have tightened but these might need to be reviewed.

3 **Housing supply**: There is a need to build more homes to address the problem of housing shortage. A significant increase in supply would reduce house prices. However, in the shorter term, there is an opportunity to make better use of existing housing stock. At present, many people might be living in properties which are unsuited to their needs – for example, older couples living in 3–4-bedroom houses. In order to free up homes for first-time buyers, some action may be required, such as a cut in stamp duty for those aged over 55 who are looking to downsize.

4 **Industry**: Sixty-three per cent of potential first-time buyers believe that relaxing borrowing rules would help redress the inequality in the homeownership market. However, these changes need to be supported by the government and regulators.

Lenders have made some changes but Santander believes they could improve in the following areas:

- Offer mortgages over longer terms
- Extend the upper age limit of mortgages
- Increase the number of people named on a mortgage
- Review what can be accepted as guarantee for deposit or loan
- Consider existing rental payments as evidence of affordability instead of using income multiples

The proposals outlined above require the government to work closely with the regulator and lenders.

Summary

The government has been helping young people climb the property ladder using measures that focus on giving a bonus on savings, interest-free loans and stamp duty exemption. All these measures are designed to deal with the problem of raising the deposit and upfront costs, and stamp duty exemption is probably the most helpful as it gives an immediate saving to all first-time buyers.

The attempt to help first-time buyers to deal with the question of affordability has not been successful. The Starter Homes Scheme (giving buyers 20 per cent discount) has not materialized, while no details have been provided for the First Homes Scheme (giving buyers £100,000 discount).

While the government has been working closely with builders, they have not worked with other stakeholders (e.g. parents, employers, lenders or regulator (FCA)) to help first-time buyers. Following the introduction of the Mortgage Market Review in 2014 by the FCA, lending criteria have become stricter, making it more difficult to obtain a mortgage. In the next chapter, we will turn to the mortgage lending criteria and challenges facing first-time buyers in getting a mortgage.

References

Bieoley, K., 2018, 'Being Single Is Costing Me a Shared Ownership Home', *Financial Times*, 12 January 2018 [online]. Available at www.ft.com/content/e151241e-f227-11e7-ac08-07c3086a2625 [Accessed 14 November 2020].

Blanden, J. and Machin, S., 2017, 'Home Ownership and Social Mobility', *CentrePiece Summer 2017* [online]. Available at https://cep.lse.ac.uk/pubs/download/cp508.pdf [Accessed 29 April 2021].

Chamberlain, Z., 2020, *This Is How Long It Takes to Get a Council House in Birmingham*, 29 February 2020 [online]. Available at www.birminghammail.co.uk/news/midlands-news/how-long-takes-council-house-17815997.

Cosslett, R.L., 2017, 'The Bank of Mum and Dad: It's Such a Huge Amount of Money And Guilt', *The Guardian* [online]. Available at www.theguardian.com/money/2017/nov/11/generation-rent-property-borrowing-from-mum-and-dad-guilt [Accessed 14 November 2020].

Disney, R., and Luo, G., 2020, 'The right to buy public housing in Britain: a welfare analysis'. Institute for Fiscal Studies, *IFS Working Paper*, W15/05 [online]. Available at www.ifs.org.uk/uploads/publications/wps/WP201505.pdf [Accessed 14 November 2020].

English Housing Survey Headline Report 2018–19 [online]. Available at https://assets.publishing.service.gov.uk/government/uploads/system/uploads/attachment_data/file/860076/2018-19_EHS_Headline_Report.pdf [Accessed 14 November 2020].

Gov. UK., 2021, *Right to Buy: Buying Your Council Home* [online]. Available at https://www.gov.uk/right-to-buy-buying-your-council-home/discounts#:~:text=You%20can%20get%20a%20discount,consumer%20price%20index%20(%20CPI%20) [Accessed 29 April 2021].

Green, N., 2020, 'How the Stamp Duty Holiday Works for Homebuyers and Landlords', *Unbiased* [online]. Available at www.unbiased.co.uk/news/mortgages/rishi-sunak-announces-stamp-duty-holiday.

HM Revenue and Customs, 2020, *Individual Savings Account (ISA) Statistics*, June 2020 [online]. Available at https://assets.publishing.service.gov.uk/government/uploads/system/uploads/attachment_data/file/894771/ISA_Statistics_Release_June_2020.pdf, p. 21 [Accessed 14 November 2020].

HM Treasury, 2015, *Help to Buy: ISA – Scheme Outline*, March 2015 [online]. Available at https://assets.publishing.service.gov.uk/government/uploads/system/uploads/attachment_data/file/413899/Help_to_Buy_ISA_Guidance.pdf [Accessed 14 November 2020].

HM Treasury, 2021, *The Mortgage Guarantee Scheme: An Outline* [online]. https://assets.publishing.service.gov.uk/government/uploads/system/uploads/attachment_data/file/965665/210301_Budget_Supplementary_Doc_-_mortgage_guarantee_scheme.pdf [Accessed 6 March 2021].

Home Owners Alliance, *No Homes Built Under Government Starter Homes Initiative*, 7 November 2019 [online]. Available at https://hoa.org.uk/2019/11/starter-homes-initiative/ [Accessed 14 November 2020].

Kentish, B., 2017, 'Forty Percent of Homes Sold Under Right to Buy Now in the Hands of Private Landlords', *The Independent*, 8 December 2017 [online]. Available at www.independent.co.uk/news/uk/politics/right-to-buy-homes-sold-private-landlords-latest-figures-rent-a8098126.html [Accessed 14 November 2020].

Lawrence, C., 2019, 'Help to Buy Is Finally Being Scrapped: Here's Why It Was a Terrible Idea', *City Metric*, 8 January 2019 [online]. Available at www.citymetric.com/politics/help-buy-finally-being-scrapped-here-s-why-it-was-terrible-idea-4419 [Accessed 14 November 2020].

Legal and General, 2019, *Bank of Mum and Dad* [Online]. Available at www.legalandgeneral.com/landg-assets/adviser/retirement/literature-and-forms/articles-and-reports/BoMaD.pdf [Accessed 14 November 2020].

Maunder, S., 2020, 'First-time Buyers Could Get a £100,000 Discount on a New Home: What's the Catch?', *Which* [online]. Available at www.which.co.uk/news/2020/02/first-time-buyers-could-get-a-100000-discount-on-a-new-home-whats-the-catch/ [Accessed 14 November 2020].

National Statistics, *Help to Buy (Equity Loan Scheme) Data to 31 March 2020* [online]. Available at https://assets.publishing.service.gov.uk/government/uploads/system/uploads/attachment_data/file/903024/Help_To_Buy_Equity_Loan_2020_Q1_Statistical_Release.pdf [Accessed 14 November 2020].

National Statistics, *Local Authority Housing Statistics: Year Ending March 2018, England*, p. 6 [Online]. Available at https://assets.publishing.service.gov.uk/government/uploads/system/uploads/attachment_data/file/773079/

Local_Authority_Housing_Statistics_England_year_ending_March_2018. pdf [Accessed 14 November 2020].

Rhodes, C., *Construction Industry: Statistics and Policy*. House of Commons Library, Briefing Paper, 16 Dec 2019, No 01432 [Online]. Available at https://commonslibrary.parliament.uk/research-briefings/sn01432/ [Accessed 14 November 2020].

Right to Buy Sales in England: October to December 2019, Released 27 March 2020 [online]. Available at https://assets.publishing.service.gov.uk/ government/uploads/system/uploads/attachment_data/file/876151/ Right_to_Buy_Sales_October_to_December_2019.pdf [Accessed 14 November 2020].

Statista, 2020, 'Population of the UK in 2019, by Age Group', *Statista* [online]. Available at www.statista.com/statistics/281174/uk-population-by-age/ [Accessed 14 November 2020].

Tilford, S., 2020, 'As the Rich Get Richer, Why Don't British People Care About Inequality?', *The Guardian* [online]. Available at www.theguardian. com/commentisfree/2018/sep/18/rich-britons-inequality-poverty-social-wealth [Accessed 14 November 2020].

UK House Price Index for January 2020 [online]. Available at www.gov.uk/ government/news/uk-house-price-index-for-january-2020#:~: text=on%20average%2C%20house%20prices%20have,UK%20valued%20 at%20%C2%A3231%2C185 [Accessed 14 November 2020].

Walker, P., 2016, 'The London Borough with a "50-year Waiting List" for Council Houses', *The Guardian*, 19 October 2016 [online]. Available at www. theguardian.com/society/2016/oct/19/council-house-wait-50-years-barking-and-dagenham-councillor-documentary-london-no-place-to-call-home [Accessed 14 November 2020].

Wilson, W., Cromarty, H., Seely, A., and Barton, C., 2021, 'Extending Home Ownership: Government Initiatives,' *House of Commons Library*, Briefing Paper, Number 03668, March 2021 [online]. Available at https://commons library.parliament.uk/research-briefings/sn03668/ [Accessed 29 April 2021].

Zoopla, 2020, *Government Home Buying Schemes Explained* [online]. Available at www.zoopla.co.uk/discover/first-time-buyers/first-time-buyer-government-scheme/ [Accessed 14 November 2020].

CHAPTER EIGHT
HOW TO GET A MORTGAGE

Buying a house often involves a large amount of money, and this means that, for many people, it is necessary to borrow to pay for the purchase. Mortgage is a type of loan used to pay for a property and it is different from other types of borrowings because a lender takes the property which it offers a loan on as security. For this reason, mortgages are also known as secured loans.

Mortgage lending provides funding for over 70 per cent of property transactions in the UK (UK Finance, 2019). This means that banks play a pivotal role in the property market, as their lending criteria determine who can obtain a mortgage and the volume of property transactions. We have seen in Chapter 7 that the government and parents also play a role in the first-time buyer property market, but this is secondary to that of banks and lenders.

The aim of this chapter is to examine the key lending criteria which can affect a buyer's ability to buy a property, different ways banks have sought to help first-time buyers get on the property ladder and strategies to repay a mortgage.

Lending criteria

When you apply for a mortgage, there are four factors that determine your ability to obtain a mortgage: availability of suitable loans, your credit profile, affordability and the suitability of the property as security.

For many buyers, especially first-time buyers, the availability of high loan to value mortgages is important because it means you only need to put down a small deposit. However, the availability of such loans is dependent on a lender's view of the future movements of the property market. If a lender believes property prices are likely to fall, they seek to reduce risks by lowering the amount of money they are willing to lend on a property. This, in turn, affects a buyer's ability to buy a property if they cannot raise the necessary deposit.

Three other factors also affect your ability to obtain a mortgage: (a) *your credit profile*, (b) *your income and expenses*, and (c) *the type of property*. Thus, a mortgage application needs to pass both tests: satisfy the lender that you can service the mortgage and that the property you have chosen will be easy to resell. We will now discuss these points in turn.

High loan-to-value mortgages

Research shows that the availability of high loan-to-value (LTV) mortgages is one of the most significant factors determining the number of first-time buyers able to buy a property. Since the early 1980s first-time buyers have tended to borrow at high LTVs (of at least 90 per cent), because they tend to be younger, have smaller savings and, unlike home

Table 8.1 Number of first-time buyers, 2008–20

Year	Number of first-time buyers
2008	192,300
2009	196,700
2010	199,400
2011	193,700
2012	217,900
2013	269,500
2014	309,100
2015	309,400
2016	337,200
2017	362,800
2018	370,000
2019	356,767
2020 (October)	354,400

Source: Halifax (2019), Green (2020)

movers and remortgagors, do not have the equity in a property they own to finance the deposit (Kuvshinov, n.d.).

The widespread availability of high LTV mortgages reflects a lender's confidence in the property market. However, in times of economic uncertainties, lenders tend to reduce the amount of loan they are willing to lend on a property due to fears of falling prices, negative equity (when the amount of mortgage is higher than the value of the property) and job losses. All of these weaken their confidence in the housing market.

The financial crisis of 2008, for example, led to the contraction of lending to first-time buyers as lenders lowered the LTV ceilings on their lending and increased the interest rate spreads on high LTV products in particular. Thus, in 2008, the number of first-time buyers fell to a lowest level with only 192,300 registered.

The number of first-time buyers began to increase noticeably after 2012, thanks to a lower rate of growth in house price, low interest rates, increase in high loan value mortgages (85–90 per cent and 90–95 per cent bands by 21.8 and 23.3 per cent, respectively) (FSA, 2012) and the introduction of stamp duty land tax relief scheme.

However, as a result of COVID-19, the number of first-time buyers appears to decrease again as lenders withdraw high LTV mortgages due to widespread fears of falling house prices and increasing job losses. According to the *Financial Times*, the number of high LTV mortgages fell from 1,172 products in September 2019 to 76 in September 2020 (Cheung, 2020). Moneyfacts Treasury Reports also confirm the drastic decline of high LTV mortgages between November 2019 and November 2020, see Table 8.2 below (Magnus, 2020).

The reduction of high LTV mortgages affects a buyer's ability to buy a property because it means that they have to find a bigger deposit. When 90 per cent LTV mortgages are available, buyers only need to find 10 per cent deposit. However, if the LTV is reduced to 75 per cent, it

Table 8.2 Number of mortgage products, 2019–20

	November 2019	March 2020	July 2020	October 2020	November 2020
Total product count – all LTVs	5,077	5,222	2,728	2,259	2,404
Product count – 90% LTV	761	779	70	51	56
Product count – 85% LTV	675	664	356	329	344

Source: Magnus (2020)

means a buyer must find a deposit equivalent to 25 per cent of the value of the property. Unless they can raise the necessary deposit, they will not be able to buy a property.

Credit scoring

After finding a suitable LTV mortgage, a borrower must pass credit scoring to proceed to the next stage. Lenders use credit scoring to decide how risky it is to lend to you. They assess risk by looking at your past financial conduct as revealed by your credit profile/record. This is a history of your past borrowings and repayments and contains information such as the amount of borrowings, any late payments and bankruptcy, and financial associations with other people. The four main credit reference agencies in the UK are Experian, Equifax, TransUnion (formerly known as Call Credit) and Crediva.

Many lenders use credit scoring to help them decide whether to lend or not. Each lender uses its own credit scoring system, but credit reference agencies make available indicative scores and their possible outcomes. In times of economic uncertainties, lenders may only accept borrowers with a score above a certain level.

There are several factors that affect your credit score.

Enhancing factors: Factors that enhance your credit score include:

- **Registration on the electoral roll**: It is important to register on the electoral roll, because it allows lenders to verify who you are and where you are living. This information can help prevent fraud and allow a lender to determine whether you have a stable life.

Registration at an address for a long time suggests that you are a lower risk borrower because you have a stable place to live. Lenders like to see signs of stability in your credit report because it indicates you are in a better position to pay back debt, and that your behaviour is not likely to change. Other signs of stability include the average age of your credit card accounts, the amount of debt that you have, how long you have a bank account and so on.

- **Credit utilization**: Credit utilization (how much of your available credit you're using) is also believed to be an important factor in determining your credit score, as this shows your financial position and dependency on credit. It is recommended that the ratio should be kept under 30 per cent. This, along with responsible behaviours like on-time payments, can help improve your credit score in the long run (Capital One, 2020).

Negative factors: Factors that affect your credit score negatively include:

- **Late payments**: lenders do not like to see late payments on your credit record because these indicate that you are not a reliable borrower, and lending to you is risky because there is no guarantee that you will pay your mortgage payments on time.
- **Application for too much credit in a short space of time**: is not desirable because it indicates that you are taking on too much debt or that you are desperate for money.
- **Maxed-out credit cards**: indicates that you might be living beyond your means and have too much debt.
- **County Court Judgement (CCJ), Individual Voluntary Arrangements (IVAs) and bankruptcies and insolvencies**: lenders see these as signs that you have not been a good borrower and therefore lending to you is a high risk. Some lenders can lend to individuals with a poor credit history, but will charge a higher interest rate. The good news is that this information will be erased from a credit profile after six years.

If you have no credit history, this also affects your credit score adversely as a lender has nothing to judge whether you will be a reliable borrower or not. It is therefore advisable to have a credit card so that you can build up your credit history but make sure you control your spending and pay off the balance every month.

> **Manual underwriting**: Some lenders do not use credit scoring to assess a mortgage application but rely on manual underwriting (e.g. an underwriter assesses your circumstances to make decisions rather than relying on an automated system). If you believe that you might have an issue with your credit profile, you may wish to use these lenders.
>
> **Tip**: If you use a mortgage adviser, they can tell you which lender is the best option for your circumstances, and which credit reference agency a prospective lender uses. You can then obtain a copy of your credit report to make sure that there are no issues before submitting your application to avoid leaving 'footprints' on your profile.

Affordability

Besides credit scoring, a lender also carries out an affordability test. Prior to the financial crisis of 2008, mortgage lenders determined the amount you could borrow by looking at your income and then multiply this by an income multiple to establish how much you could borrow. On paper, the lending criteria were strict as you typically could only borrow on average 3–3.5 times your salary, although some specialist lenders could go up to five times your income.

However, in practice, lending was easier as there were self-certification mortgages where you did not need to provide proof of your income. Self-certified mortgages were blamed for the financial problems that led to the financial crisis of 2008 and were subsequently banned in 2016.

Borrowing to buy a property is much harder now because of the changes in the way in which lenders assess how much you can afford to borrow. In the past, lenders focused predominantly on your income to determine how much you could borrow. Now they need to consider also your expenses and the effect of a possible interest rate rise on your future ability to meet mortgage commitments. If a lender believes you will not be able to afford your mortgage payments in these circum-stances, they might limit how much you can borrow.

When working out how much you can afford to borrow, a lender will look at:

Your income

- your basic income
- income from your pension or investments
- income in the form of child maintenance and financial support from ex-spouses
- any other earnings you have – for example, from overtime, commission or bonus payments or a second job or freelance work. However, as this income is not guaranteed, a lender may only accept a proportion.

You will need to provide payslips and bank statements as evidence of your income.

If you're self-employed, you'll need to provide:

- bank statements
- business accounts (three years)
- details of the income tax you've paid.

Your outgoings

Lenders now also rigorously check your outgoings to determine affordability, such as

- credit card repayments
- maintenance payments
- insurance – building, contents, travel, pet, life, etc.
- any other loans or credit agreements you might have
- bills such as water, gas, electricity, phone, broadband.

They might ask for estimates of your living costs such as spending on clothes, basic recreation and childcare. They might also request to see some recent bank statements to back up the figures you supply.

It is therefore important to minimise unsecured debt such as credit card, hire purchase, overdraft and personal loan so that you can borrow more.

Future changes that might make an impact

In addition, a lender needs to consider possible changes on your ability to pay your mortgage, such as an interest rate increase. In 2014, the Financial Policy Committee (FPC) (part of the Bank of England) introduced new rules, including a requirement for mortgage lenders to stress test mortgage affordability. Mortgage lenders need to ensure that new mortgage borrowers could afford their mortgage payments if interest rates went up by 3 per cent above their standard variable rate within the first five years of the loan. For example, a lender offers an introductory deal at 1 per cent and its standard variable rate is 4.74 per cent. Under the new regulations imposed by the Bank of England, a lender needs to ensure that borrowers can afford to repay the mortgage based on an interest rate of 3 per cent above the standard variable rate: 4.74 per cent + 3 per cent = 7.74 per cent.

However, long-term fixed-rate mortgages (five years or more) are not covered by the mortgage affordability rules, and lenders do not need to stress test borrowers taking out these deals. This, along with low interest rates, contribute to a growing popularity of long-term fixed-rate mortgages (Bank of England, 2020).

Ways to help first-time buyers when income insufficient

Affordability is one of the main barriers for young people to get on the property ladder, due to the fact that property prices have been risen faster than wages, and that many young people are not earning a salary high enough. An average property in the UK costs £231,000 in March 2021. Based on 4.5 times income multiple and a 95 per cent mortgage, this means that a borrower needs to have a salary of £49,000. However, the average salary in the UK is £28,500, and so this means that two borrowers or more are required on the mortgage.

Lenders are aware that inadequate income is a real challenge for some prospective buyers and offer some innovative mortgage products to deal with the problem.

Increase your income

A first obvious solution is to increase your income by earning more. Lenders will accept all incomes, including a second job, commission and over-time. However, the percentage of these incomes they can accept varies from lender to lender. The Halifax, for example, used to accept 60 per cent of overtime income but has now reduced to 30 per cent during the pandemic crisis.

Buy a property with someone

A second solution is to buy a property with someone so that you can use more than one income in your mortgage application. Lenders allow up to four people to be named on a mortgage, but many only allow two incomes to be used in the assessment. In 2018–19, half (49 per cent) of first-time buyers bought their first home jointly with a partner or spouse while 47 per cent bought in their name only (English Housing Survey, 2018–19). The trend is that many are buying jointly with someone.

Some banks accept incomes of all applicants named on the mortgage. The Metro Bank, for examples, takes the income of all applicants and thus a maximum of four incomes can be used. Parents, for example, can have a mortgage with their son/daughter.

Rent a room mortgages

Some specialist lenders offer this innovative mortgage whereby they will consider potential rental income you might get if you were to rent out a room in the house you are buying. Imagine you buy a three-bedroom house and only use one room. You can potentially rent out two rooms to earn extra income. A specialist lender will add this potential income to your salary to decide how much you can borrow.

In the UK, rent a room relief lets you receive up to £7,500 in rent each year from a lodger, tax-free. However, this only applies if you rent out furnished accommodation in your own home.

This type of mortgage is only available from specialist lenders. It appears that Bath Building Society is one of the few who offer this product. The rates therefore are not as competitive as a mortgage from a high street bank. However, during COVID-19 this product was withdrawn.

Borrow your parents' names – joint borrower, sole proprietor mortgage

Another solution is to buy a property jointly with your parents and use their income for mortgage assessment. Thus, first-time buyers can now add their parents to the mortgage application, as parents normally have a higher income, and this type of mortgage is known as 'joint borrower, sole proprietor', or JBSP mortgages.

This type of mortgage is becoming popular because the child can get on the property ladder even if they have no salary or income. The child also qualifies for first-time buyer stamp duty exemptions, while the parents avoid paying the additional 3 per cent stamp duty surcharge on a second home. In addition, the parents can avoid paying capital gains tax on any increase in the value of the house when it is sold and do not need to worry about inheritance tax as they do not own a share of the property. This means that parents can buy a property jointly with their child when they are at university and enjoy high street lender rates.

JBSP mortgages are a niche product and are only offered by a limited number of lenders. Around 12 lenders offer these mortgages, including high street banks such as Barclays, Metro, Clydesdale, along with building societies such as Skipton, Newcastle, Hinckley & Rugby and Buckinghamshire. Interest rates are typically the same as with a regular mortgage (Vaidya, 2020).

The main disadvantage of this type of mortgage is that the length of the mortgage might be very short, as this is determined by the age of the parents. Because of a shorter period of time to repay the loan, monthly mortgage payments might be unaffordable. The loan has to be repaid on a repayment basis (pay interest and capital) and so monthly payments tend to be higher.

This mortgage also requires the parents to earn a salary high enough to cover two mortgages – their own mortgage and the new one for their child. In addition, the amount of the new loan will be affected by the value of the mortgage the parents already have. If the parents have a high income and an unencumbered (no mortgage) property, this might not present a problem. However, if they have a high mortgage balance, they may not be able to borrow the amount needed.

Acceptable properties as security

After satisfying that you can afford your monthly mortgage payments, a lender needs to make sure that the property is suitable as a security for the loan. They send out surveyors to value and assess the property.

Surveyors offer three types of survey:

1   **Basic mortgage valuation** to assess whether the property is a suitable security for mortgage lending purposes. The report is therefore very basic.
2   **Homebuyer's report** is designed to give the buyer an opinion on the condition of the property. This report is more detailed.
3   **Structural report** highlights any structural problems. A structural report is the most expensive and protects buyers from any negligence (e.g. failure to report any problems with the property). In order words, buyers can sue surveyors for damages if they are found to be negligent later. This is the most detailed and expensive.

Standard construction

Choosing the right type of property to buy is important because it will determine whether it is easy to get a mortgage and insurance and what interest rates you need to pay. If you buy a property that you can get a mortgage from most lenders, you avoid paying high interest rates and expensive insurance. It also means it will be easier to sell your property in the future.

Lenders prefer property of standard construction over non-standard. Standard construction means the property is normally built with brick or stone, and the roof is made of slate or tile. A non-standard construction is therefore anything that falls outside of this and includes timber framed houses, log-style cabins and prefabricated concrete houses.

It is possible to get a mortgage on non-standard properties but you might need to approach a specialist lender. The consumer magazine **Which** has identified 16 different types of property which is more difficult to obtain a mortgage including, ex-local authority housing – especially high-rise flats, properties made of concrete, flats above a shop or commercial premise, studio flats, freehold flats, properties with short leases and properties not in a habitable condition (Horne, 2019).

As non-standard construction properties carry a greater risk, lenders often charge a higher interest rate and restrict the LTV to ensure that the mortgage does not exceed the value of the property. To minimize risks, it is advisable to buy a standard property as it is easier to get a mortgage and re-sell.

Mortgages

Households normally rely on mortgages to assist them to buy a property. Although a house purchase is often the largest single purchase and one of the most significant financial decisions, many people do not spend enough time searching for a mortgage. As a result, many prospective buyers make difficult mortgage-related decisions with minimal guidance and consideration.

In choosing a mortgage, a prospective buyer needs to think about some of these difficult decisions:

1   How to repay a mortgage
2   How much deposit to put down
3   What is the best type of mortgage
4   What is the optimal term for a mortgage
5   Is it better to go for two, three, five years or longer mortgage deals
6   Are mortgages with a low interest rate and high fees better than those with a high interest rate and low fees

We will discuss these issues in turn.

How to repay a mortgage

When you take out a mortgage, you'll have to pay back two elements: the lump sum (known as the principal) and interest on the loan.

A lender might offer you two ways to repay the loan: capital and interest mortgage (also known as repayment mortgage) and interest-only mortgage. An interest-only mortgage means that you only pay the interest on the loan, not the amount borrowed. The mortgage amount remains level throughout the term, as you have not repaid any of the capital borrowed, as shown in Figure 8.1. Although this makes monthly payment more affordable, you still have to repay the loan at the end of the term.

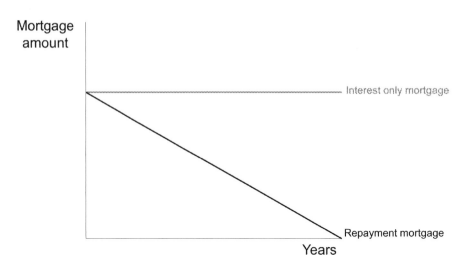

Figure 8.1 Interest and repayment mortgage

For example, you take out a mortgage for £100,000 over 25 years. If you go for an interest-only mortgage, you still owe £100,000 at the end of 25 years because you have only paid the interest on the loan and not the debt (e.g. £100,000). If you go for a repayment mortgage, you will owe the house outright at the end of 25 years because you have paid off the loan and any interest charged.

There are several reasons why some borrowers might opt for an interest-only mortgage. Firstly, the monthly payment is lower than the monthly payment on a repayment mortgage because you do not pay off the amount you borrow. This might be attractive to those borrowers who expect their financial situation to improve (e.g. through promotion, inheritance).

Secondly, interest-only mortgages are widely accepted on properties which are rented out. Since the owner does not live in the property, they can always sell the property at the end of the term to repay the loan.

Thirdly, some borrowers might opt for an interest-only mortgage because they might be able to get a better return by investing the difference in monthly payments. A monthly payment on a repayment mortgage is around 30 per cent higher than an interest-only mortgage monthly payment. By investing the difference in monthly payments in investment vehicles such as ISAs, borrowers can accumulate a lump sum to repay the mortgage. Obviously, this is a riskier method and does not guarantee that the mortgage will be paid off at the end of the term.

Since the 2008 financial crisis, lenders have become stricter and require borrowers to repay both capital and interest on residential mortgages (those for owners to live in). The English Housing Survey found that 98 per cent of first-time buyers have a repayment mortgage in 2018–19. Interest-only mortgages are only permitted in special circumstances, such as those who can prove that they have other assets (e.g. wealth from other properties) which they can use to repay the loan at the end of the mortgage term. This, in effect, rules out interest-only mortgages for first-time buyers.

A repayment mortgage, on the other hand, guarantees that the mortgage is repaid at the end of the term because each monthly mortgage payment is allocated in two ways:

- a portion goes to pay the simple interest on outstanding debt
- the remainder goes to repay a portion of the principal

It is a risk-free, straightforward and guaranteed method to repay the mortgage. Based on the interest rate and term of the mortgage chosen, the lender works out how much you need to pay monthly to ensure that the loan will be paid off. In early years of a mortgage, a large part of the monthly payment is made up of the interest element, but as the years progress, a greater proportion goes towards the repayment of the principal.

As the amount of outstanding debt is reduced, the portion of the payment to pay interest decreases while the part devoted to the principal increases. It takes many years of monthly payments to significantly reduce the outstanding balance of the loan.

As the loan is slowly being repaid, the homeowner gradually builds up their equity. Homeowner's equity represents the amount that has been paid off plus any appreciation in the value of the property. The equity portion of a mortgage payment is a type of forced savings and explains why homeowners typically have a higher net worth than renters. Overpaying on a mortgage thus represents one way of saving.

How much deposit should be put down?

How much deposit you put down affects the loan to value, and this in turn can affect your monthly mortgage payments. A lower LTV mortgage carries a lower risk and may qualify for preferential rates. Since the financial crisis in 2008, lenders in the UK have sought to reduce their risk by charging different interest rates on different loans to value.

A loan with a lower LTV (e.g. 50 per cent or 60 per cent of the value of the property) is a lower risk than a loan that has a high LTV (90 to 95 per cent). If the value of the property fluctuates and the borrower defaults, there is a greater likelihood of getting the money back in a lower LTV mortgage than a higher LTV. Borrowers with a lower LTV, then, are offered a much better interest rate on their mortgage.

What is the best type of mortgage?

After deciding how to repay the principal, a second important decision facing borrowers is how to repay the interest charged on the amount borrowed. Mortgage payments often are the largest monthly expense and the type of mortgage deal chosen can have a huge impact.

Lenders offer several types of mortgages: fixed-rate, tracker, discounted, variable rate and offset mortgages. We will now discuss the pros and cons of each type.

Fixed-rate mortgages

A fixed-rate mortgage is often attractive to first-time buyers as it offers certainty and security. As the interest rate chosen does not change during the fixed period, a fixed-rate mortgage makes it easier to budget as borrowers know how much their monthly mortgage payments are. This type of mortgage is attractive in periods when rates are expected to rise.

The main disadvantages of a fixed-rate mortgage are that the rates can be higher than other types of mortgages, and they often have an early redemption penalty (e.g. a fine for changing, moving or repaying the mortgage early). This is often charged as a percentage of the amount borrowed, and so can be a substantial sum. For example, if you have a £100,000 mortgage with 3 per cent penalty, then you will need to pay £3,000 if you repay the mortgage. A penalty might be charged on a flat rate (e.g. 3 per cent if you repay at any time during the fixed period) or descending scale (e.g. 3 per cent in year 1, 2 per cent in year 2 and 1 per cent in year 3). A fixed-rate mortgage therefore is less flexible and does not easily accommodate a change in personal circumstance.

You need to choose a mortgage with special care, as getting out of this type of deal can be extremely expensive. Years ago, we met a lady who had a fixed-rate mortgage and had to pay £28,000 in penalty because she needed to move her mortgage to another lender to raise money on her property.

Tracker mortgages

A tracker-rate mortgage is a mortgage with an interest rate normally linked to the Bank of England base rate. A lender often charges a loading on top of the Bank of England base rate (e.g. 0.5 per cent + BoE base rate) and the interest rate will move in line with changes in the base rate.

This type of mortgage is particularly attractive when rates are expected to fall. Lenders can offer tracker-rate mortgages with or without early redemption penalty. Taking out a tracker-rate mortgage with no early redemption penalty gives you the freedom to switch to a fixed-rate mortgage when rates are expected to rise.

Discounted mortgages

Lenders also offer discounted mortgages. These are mortgages which enjoy a discount off the lender's variable rate for a fixed period of time and again many of them have an early redemption penalty. Once your initial deal ends, you may need to change your deal (and pay a fee to the lender to change).

Variable rate mortgages

A standard variable rate mortgage offers you the most flexibility as they do not have an early redemption penalty. In other words, borrowers can change, move or pay off their mortgage at any time without paying a penalty. For this flexibility, you often have to pay an interest rate which is higher than other deals available.

Many borrowers allow their mortgages to lapse to the standard variable rate, often without realising it or knowing that they have a better alternative. As a result, thousands of homeowners may be paying as much as £4,080 of additional interest each year by not switching to a better deal (Green, 2021).

Offset mortgages

Offset mortgages are less well-known than other types of mortgages and are designed to allow you to offset savings against borrowings. You might have a savings and a mortgage account with the same lender. In other words, you might lend and borrow at the same time.

An offset mortgage allows you to pay interest only on the net amount borrowed, as the lender deducts the amount of savings you have from the mortgage amount borrowed, and only charges interest on the difference. For example, you might borrow £100,000 from the lender but might have £5,000 in a savings account. Having an offset mortgage means that you only pay interest on the differential amount (£95,000).

An offset mortgage is attractive in several ways. Firstly, it is tax efficient because you do not earn any interest on your savings as you offset this against the cost of the mortgage and therefore do not pay any tax on the interest earned.

Secondly, you receive the same rate of interest on your savings as you pay on your mortgage. Lenders often charge a higher interest rate on mortgages and pay a lower interest rate on savings. In an offset mortgage, the amount of savings is deducted from the mortgage loan, and so in effect the borrowers receive the same interest rate on their savings as they pay on their mortgage.

An offset mortgage can help you pay off the loan quickly and save you a lot of money. Unfortunately, few lenders offer offset facilities.

Table 8.3 Pros and cons of different types of mortgages

Types of mortgage	Advantages	Disadvantages
Tracker	Transparency if linked to Bank of England base rate Benefit from rate reductions if rates fall	No certainty as rates can go up
Discounted	Discounts on interest rate	Early redemption penalty
Variable	Flexibility and freedom to move your mortgage	Rates tend to be higher than other deals
Fixed	Certainty Makes budgeting easier Protection against interest rate rises	Early redemption penalty No flexibility during fixed period
Offset	Reduce term of mortgage Tax efficiency Interest rate on savings same as mortgage	Rates might be higher Limited choice of lenders Need to have savings

Mortgage terms – 2, 3, 5, or longer

Many mortgage deals in the UK tend to be two, three, and five years. Whether you should go for a two- or five-year deal depends on many considerations, including:

- Your future plans: How long do you plan to live in the property? Are you likely to move to a bigger property in a few years? Will you likely to move job and place of work in the future?
- What is your appetite for risk?

Low rates and high fees, or high rates and no or low fees mortgage products

Borrowers also have to make a difficult decision of whether to choose a mortgage product with a low interest rate with a high fee, or a higher interest rate with a low fee (Gardner and Clark, 2003). In January 2021, a UK lender offers the following deals on a repayment basis to first-time buyers. The following example is based on a loan of £170,000 (85 per cent LTV) on a property worth £200,000.

In looking at these deals, a borrower needs to make two important decisions. The first decision is whether a borrower wants a product with or without early repayment charge – this is penalty for repaying the whole loan before the expiry of the deal (in this case, it is 31/3/2023).

Table 8.4 Pros and cons of different mortgage terms

Term	2 years	3 years	5 years
Advantages	Good option if circumstances are likely to change in the medium term Might be cheaper than longer deal	Compromise between 2- and 5-year deals – not too long and not too short	Security over a long period of time If rates are low, one can enjoy them for longer.
Disadvantages	Short term and need to take out another deal sooner. More fees	Short term and need to take out another deal sooner More fees	High early repayment charge if circumstances change Rates might be higher than shorter term deals

Table 8.5 Low rates high fees, or high rates low fees

Rate	APRC	Loan-to-value	Early repayment charge	Monthly payment excluding fees	Product fee
3.19% – fixed to 31/3/23	4.3	85%	Y	£824	£999
3.65% – fixed to 31/3/23	4.3	85%	Y	£865	£0
3.65% – flex fixed to 31/3/23	4.3	85%	N	£865	£499

A product without an early repayment charge is useful in several scenarios:

1 If an individual wants to overpay their monthly mortgage payment by more than the normal limit permitted (lenders normally allow borrowers to overpay by 10 per cent of the mortgage balance)
2 If interest rates are likely to drop and a borrower may wish to move to a cheaper deal
3 If a borrower may move, sell their property and repay the whole loan

A mortgage product with no early repayment penalty offers flexibility, choice and freedom, and may be worth considering when the future is uncertain. In this example, a fixed product with no early repayment penalty is in many ways ideal because it gives an individual both certainty and flexibility.

A second decision is whether an individual should opt for a lower interest rate product with a high fee or for a higher interest rate product with no fee. In this case, a borrower is offered two choices: 3.19 per cent fixed with £999 fee or 3.65 per cent fixed with no fee.

There are several factors that can help an individual making this decision:

a) **How long does it take to recover the fee?** In the example given above, the saving between the two deals (3.19 and 3.65 per cent) is £41 per month, giving a total saving over two years of £984. Once interest is added to the cost, the monthly saving will be less. In this case, the total saving in reduced monthly payments is lower than the fee charged, and therefore it is better to go for a higher interest rate and no fee product.
b) **Size of the loan**: The size of the loan affects the monthly savings. For example, if the loan is £255,000 rather than £170,000, an individual

would save £63 per month, giving a total savings of £1,512 over two years. In this case, the savings are greater than the fee and therefore a higher fee is worth considering when the loan is large.

c) **Investment returns**: Another consideration is the rate of return an individual could earn if they invested the fee. If an individual invests £999 fee, how much return could they get in two years? If an individual has a low-risk appetite and is unlikely to get a high return, then a low or no fee option is preferable.

d) **Financial discipline**: The other factor to take into account is financial discipline. Most lenders allow fees to be added to the loan, and so the mortgage amount borrowed increases and interest is payable on the fee as well. If an individual goes for a lower rate with a high fee, they will save on their monthly mortgage payment. However, whether this is a good option depends on an individual's financial circumstances and how the monthly saving is used – is the money to be invested or spent? Without financial discipline, the monthly savings are likely to be spent. However, if an individual can make a good use of this surplus income, then a high fee option is worth considering.

What is the optimal term of mortgage?

The fourth decision a borrower has to decide is the term of the mortgage – that is, how long they should borrow the money for.

Borrowers traditionally have gone for a 25 years mortgage, but lenders increasingly offer a maximum term of 40 years. The English Housing Survey shows that of those first-time buyers who had a mortgage in 2018–19, nearly half opted for a repayment term of more than 30 years, and a further half for a term between 20 and 29 years. Only a small percentage (6 per cent) went for a shorter term of 1–19 years.

Table 8.6 Popular terms of mortgages

Term of mortgage	Percentage
30 years or more	45%
20–29 years	49%
1–19 years	6%

Source: English Housing Survey, Headline Report (2018–19, p. 13)

In an article on 'Is a 30 Year Mortgage Preferable to a 15 Year Mortgage?', Basciano, Grayson and Walton argue that taking out a 30-year mortgage with a simultaneous investment plan (e.g. a lower monthly mortgage payment due to longer term and invest the difference) can bring better financial results to some borrowers than a 15-year mortgage term and a subsequent investment plan (i.e pay off mortgage first and invest afterwards), when interest rates are low and an individual has the financial discipline to invest. However, a major disadvantage with this approach is that it requires an individual to take risks, as they need to invest to produce a better financial outcome (Basciano et al., 2006, p. 20).

Although the main advantage of spreading the loan over a longer period of time is a lower monthly payment and greater affordability, a shorter term of repayment has several advantages. Firstly, the total interest paid will be lower. For example, if you borrow £100,000 and repay over 20 years instead of 25 years, you save £5,744 in interest. If you repay over 15 years instead of 25, you save a total of £11,325 in interest.

Shorter-term repayment also has other advantages, including a faster build-up of equity in the property and a forced method of saving. After the debt is paid off, an individual can enjoy a feeling of financial security and freedom as a result of having no mortgage. However, a shorter term can result in a high monthly mortgage payment, and put individuals under financial pressure.

A better solution is to opt for a longer repayment period and use other methods to pay off the loan early. This reduces financial pressure and makes faster payoff optional rather than mandatory.

A first way to pay off a mortgage quickly is to offset the costs of borrowing against the interest you earn on your savings. An offset mortgage works by allowing you to offset the cost of interest paid on the mortgage account against the interest earned on your saving account.

Table 8.7 Interest charged and term of mortgage based on £100,000 mortgage

Interest rate (%)	Term of mortgage	Monthly mortgage	Total cost	Interest charged
2	25 years	£423	£127,156	£27,156
2	20 years	£505	£121,412	£21,412
2	15 years	£643	£115,831	£15,831
2	10 years	£920	£110,416	£10,416

Source: Which mortgage repayment calculator, available at www.which.co.uk/money/mortgages-and-property/mortgage-calculators/mortgage-repayment-calculator-agbgh7r3bfhm

The additional benefit is you receive the same level of interest on savings as the rate they pay on your mortgage.

Let's assume you take out a mortgage of £100,000 over 25 years at 2 per cent interest rate. You have £1,000 in savings and save £100 every month. Table 8.8 below shows the benefit of having an offset mortgage over a standard mortgage, a saving of £9,064.

A second method is to pay more than the required monthly amount. Any over-payment can help you reduce the period you borrow money and save you interest. Most lenders allow borrowers to overpay by 10 per cent of the balance of the mortgage every year. If you borrow £100,000, for example, a lender might allow you to pay back £10,000 per year even in a mortgage with early redemption penalty.

Instead of paying off a lump sum, you can also overpay an extra amount every month. Let's assume that you have a mortgage with a balance of £100,000, you pay interest rate of 2.0 per cent and you borrow over 25 years term. The following table shows the effects of overpayment.

If you overpay £100 per month (£1,200 per year), you will shorten the period you borrow money by five years and ten months and save £6,689 in interest. If you overpay £250 per month, you will shorten the period of borrowing by ten years and nine months, and save over

Table 8.8 Standard and offset mortgage compared

	Standard mortgage + savings	*Offset mortgage*
Interest charged over 25 years	£27,156	£17,693
Interest on savings	£399	£0
Total interest charged	£26,757	£17,693

Source: L&C Mortgages, 'Offset Calculator', available at www.landc.co.uk/calculators/offset-mortgage-calculator/

Table 8.9 Effects of overpayment assuming £100,000 mortgage over 25 years at 2% interest rate

Amount of monthly overpayment	*Amount of interest saved over the term of mortgage*	*Number of years to pay off mortgage*
£100	£6,689	19 years 2 months
£150	£8,924	17 years 2 months
£200	£10,714	15 years 7 months
£250	£12,182	14 years 3 months

Source: *Which* Mortgage overpayment calculator, available at www.which.co.uk/money/mortgages-and-property/mortgage-calculators/mortgage-overpayment-calculator-a9yck2y3xs7d

£12,182 in interest. In other words, you will repay the loan in 14 years and three months, instead of 25 years. Once you have paid off the mortgage, you will enjoy living in your home without a mortgage having peace of mind and financial security.

Porting

One problem a borrower might face is that they might need to sell and move due to relocation. Many lenders are aware of this potential problem and offer borrowers the opportunity to take the mortgage to another property, known as porting. If a borrower has a fixed-rate mortgage, porting avoids the cost of penalty if a buyer needs to sell and buy something else. However, a lender may still need to carry out checks and further underwriting to ensure that you can still afford the mortgage.

Summary

A mortgage is often repaid over a long period of time (20–40 years). During this period, our health can change and this in turn can affect our ability to work, earn a living and meet our monthly mortgage commitments. The next chapter looks at your mortgage obligations, while Chapter 10 discusses steps you can take to protect you and your family from losing your home as a result of your inability to meet your mortgage commitments.

References

Bank of England, 2020, *Why Are More Borrowers Choosing Long-Term Fixed-Rate Mortgage Pproducts* [online]. Available at https://www.bankofengland.co.uk/bank-overground/2020/why-are-more-borrowers-choosing-long-term-fixed-rate-mortgage-products [Accessed 3 May 2021].

Basciano, P.B., Grayson, J.M., and Walton, J., 2006, 'Is the Thirty Year Mortgage Preferable to a Fifteen Year Mortgage?', *Financial Counseling and Planning*, 17(1), pp. 14–21.

Capital One, 2020, *Do Credit Limit Increases Hurt Your Credit Score?* [online]. Available at www.capitalone.com/learn-grow/money-management/credit-limit-increase-affect-credit-score/.

Cheung, C., 2020, 'High LTV Mortgages Down 94% Year-on-year', *Financial Times* [online]. Available at www.ftadviser.com/mortgages/2020/09/08/high-ltv-mortgages-down-94-year-on-year/?page=1 [Accessed 18 November 2020].

English Housing Surveys, 2018–19, p. 13, p. 15 [online]. Available at https://assets.publishing.service.gov.uk/government/uploads/system/uploads/attachment_data/file/860076/2018-19_EHS_Headline_Report.pdf [Accessed 17 November 2020].

FSA, 2012, *Mortgages Product Sales Data (PSD) Trend Report | 2005–2012* [online]. Available at www.fca.org.uk/publication/data/fsa-psd-mortgages-2012.pdf [Accessed 18 November 2020].

Gardner, R., and Clark, J., 2003, 'The Decision to Pay Points When Borrowing', *Journal of Financial Planning*, 16(4), pp. 80–87.

Green, N., 2020, 'Decade Trend Gives Hope to First-time Buyers', *Unbiased* [online]. Available at www.unbiased.co.uk/news/mortgages/decade-trend-gives-hope-to-first-time-buyers [Accessed 23 November 2020].

Green, N., 2021, 'SVR Mortgage Confusion Costs Homeowners Over £4k', *Unbiased* [online]. Available at https://www.unbiased.co.uk/news/mortgages/svr-mortgage-confusion-costs-homeowners-over-4k [Accessed 29 April 2021].

Halifax, 2019, *First-time Buyers Make up Biggest Part of Property Market for First-Time in 23 Years* [online]. Available at www.lloydsbankinggroup.com/globalassets/documents/media/press-releases/halifax/2019/190223-halifax-first-time-buyer-review_final.pdf [Accessed 18 November 2020].

Horne, B., 2019, 'Revealed: 16 Homes to Avoid If You Want to Get a Mortgage', *Which* [online]. Available at www.which.co.uk/news/2019/02/revealed-16-homes-to-avoid-if-you-want-to-get-a-mortgage/ [Accessed 17 November 2020].

Kuvshinov, D., n.d., 'Recent Trends in the UK First-time Buyer Mortgage Market', *IFC Bulletin No 34*, pp. 599–610 [online]. Available at www.bis.org/ifc/publ/ifcb34aq.pdf [Accessed 18 November 2020].

L&C Mortgages, 2021, *Offset Calculator* [online]. Available at www.landc.co.uk/calculators/offset-mortgage-calculator/

Magnus, E., 2020, 'A Tale of Two Housing Markets: Equity-rich Homeowners See Mortgage Rates Plummet as First-time Buyers Watch Rates Climb and 90% Almost Vanish', *Thisismoney*, 13 November 2020 [online]. Available at www.thisismoney.co.uk/money/mortgageshome/article-8929545/Mortgage-rates-plummet-lots-equity-90-cent-mortgages-expensive.html [Accessed 23 November 2020].

UK Finance, 2019, *The Changing Shape of the UK Mortgage Market* [online]. Available at www.ukfinance.org.uk/system/files/The-changing-shape-of-the-UK-mortgage-market-FINAL-ONLINE-Jan-2020.pdf [Accessed 18 November 2020].

Vaidya, N., 2020, 'Joint Borrower Sole Proprietor Mortgage', *Money* [online]. Available at https://www.money.co.uk/mortgages/guides/joint-borrower-sole-proprietor-mortgages [Accessed 29 April 2021].

CHAPTER NINE

UNDERSTAND YOUR LEGAL RIGHTS AND OBLIGATIONS

Homeownership is associated with pride, higher self-esteem, better life satisfaction and increased psychological well-being. However, buying a property often requires you to take out a mortgage, but this can make you feel insecure, anxious, fearful and stressed, as the amount involved is often large, and the time frame to repay the debt is very long, usually 25 years or more. Yet, the future is full of uncertainties and many life events (e.g. unemployment and poor health) can happen, affecting your ability to earn a living and fulfil your mortgage commitments.

The fear of not being able to keep up with mortgage payments is a source of great anxiety for many because the lender has the power to take your property and make you homeless. When you take out a mortgage, you offer the lender your property as security, typically in the form of a deed. This gives the lender a *lien* on the property, allowing them to repossess and sell it in the event the borrower defaults on the loan. For this reason, some people argue that those who own a property with a mortgage are not real homeowners because they can lose their home if they cannot pay their mortgage payments. It is suggested that the term *homeowner* should only be used to describe those who own their home outright without a mortgage.

The prospect of losing one's home in the UK is very real. The Money Charity reports that 14 properties are repossessed every day

Table 9.1 Repossessions in UK, 1970–2019

Years	Number of repossessions
1970–79	34,370
1980–89	140,150
1990–99	425,800
2000–09	220,100
2010–19	193,070

Source: 'Repossession statistics, 1969–2019', www.ticfinance.co.uk

in England and Wales (one every 1 hour and 40 minutes). Every year 100,000 families are expected to lose their homes due to missed mortgage payments.

The 1990s saw the highest number of repossessions, due to high interest rates. Since 2009, interest rate has been low and the number of repossessions has halved, with a total of 193,070.

The good news is that the number of repossessions has steadily declined in recent years and has reached one of the lowest levels. The number of repossessions in the UK peaked in 1991 with 75,500, then fell steadily before picking up again with the onset of the financial crisis in 2009 with 48,900. Since 2015, the number of repossessions has fallen from 10,200 to reach just over 4,500 in 2019. This represents one of the lowest number of repossessions in the UK since 1969 (Money Charity, 2020, TIC Finance).

The fear of losing one's home means that stress levels among homeowners with a mortgage are reported to be higher than those without a mortgage, because as long as they have a mortgage, they always have a fear of losing their home. Repossession is distressing because it entails the loss of not only life savings (e.g. the deposit) but also pride and a home. However, homeowners with a mortgage are still in a better position than renters who experience more stress (Cairney and Boyle, 2004; Rohe et al., 2001).

The courts recognize that being forced out of one's home is a distressing experience for those involved. For this reason, they are reluctant to grant repossession orders and encourage lenders to give homeowners as many opportunities as possible to avoid this.

This chapter discusses the legal obligations on a borrower, the consequences of not being able to pay mortgage payments and the steps a lender must follow to repossess a property.

Pay back the loan, pay interest and any associated fees/charges

One of the key conditions of a mortgage is the obligation to pay back the loan, and any associated interest, charges and costs. Details of these, along with a schedule of monthly payments, are outlined in a mortgage offer.

Mortgage payments are *priority* debts and must be paid before other types of debt. Payments are collected monthly via direct debit, allowing lenders to adjust monthly payments if necessary. Lenders often ask you for your preference of the date of the direct debit and this can be done at the application stage. If not, you can speak to the lender and agree or change the date when the direct debit is paid.

Lenders can sometimes permit you to stop or reduce your monthly payments or have a payment holiday. For example, during COVID-19, lenders approved more than 2 million mortgage payment deferrals to customers and buy-to-let landlords where their ability to meet their monthly mortgage payments was impacted by the pandemic (UK Finance, 2020). It is unclear whether this is a sign that some property owners do not have a financial buffer to protect them against unforeseen circumstances, or a desire to take advantage of the opportunity to build up cash reserve during times of economic uncertainty.

Mortgage arrears

The first step towards repossession is falling behind with mortgage payments and building up mortgage arrears. In the UK, there were 11 million households with an average mortgage debt of £132,242 in January 2020. However, a small percentage of households (1.5 per cent) have difficulties paying their mortgage. At the end of December 2020, a total of 167,993 households had mortgage arrears equivalent to 1.5 per cent of their outstanding mortgage balance. Of these, 73,580 had arrears equivalent to 2.5 per cent while 22,840 with arrears equivalent to 10 per cent of the value of their mortgage, as can be seen in Table 9.2 (Money Charity, 2020, p. 9). Households with a high percentage in arrears show that they face a sustained struggle to keep their 'head above water'.

It appears that the number of mortgages with arrears is slowly rising. According to the FCA, the number of mortgages with arrears rose from approximately 170,000 in Quarter 4 in 2019 to 196,000 by Quarter 2 2020, with the amount of arrears increased from £13,425 millions to

Table 9.2 Mortgage arrears 2020

Arrears as percentage of outstanding mortgage	1.5%	2.5%	10%
Number with arrears	167,993	73,580	22,840
% of total 11 million with mortgage	1.5%	0.67%	0.2%

Source: Money Charity (March 2020, pp. 9, 13)

£14,052 millions. This represents less than one per cent of the total loan balance (FCA, September 2020, Summary 3).

Mortgage arrears are reported to be the biggest source of debt in households across the UK. In 2018, the average arrears amount was a total of £3,581. Unless action is taken, persistent arrears increase the risk of repossession (Cadle, 2018).

Reasons for late payments/arrears/problems paying your mortgage

Research shows that there are three different types of factors that make people fall behind with their mortgage payments and go into arrears.

1   *Structural factors*: changes in income/loan ratios, interest rates, government subsidies, social security support levels and loan/value ratios can affect a household's ability to pay its mortgage payments.
2   *Household income and expenditure factors*: changes in a household's income and expenses can also affect its ability to meet mortgage payments. Households may see their income goes down because of unemployment, short-term working, marital breakdown and sickness, while its expenses go up because of unanticipated repairs and other household expenditure and loan repayments.
3   *Personal factors*: a household's response to changes in its household income and expenses is critical, and its money management skills and commitment to keep the house can determine the outcome. For example, a fall of income does not necessarily result in mortgage arrears because a household can respond by cutting down its unnecessary expenses to save money.

It is found that the common reasons which lead people to fall behind with their mortgage payments include redundancy, drop in earnings, small business failures and relationship breakdown (Nettleton and Burrows, 1998, p. 735).

This suggests that mortgages are built on flawed assumptions. Firstly, mortgages are built on the assumption that people have stable employment over the life of their mortgage. However, the increasing prevalence of zero and short-term employment contracts and self-employment rates make it difficult for many to obtain a stable income to meet their mortgage obligations.

Secondly, mortgages also assume that those with a mortgage enjoy good health over the term of the mortgage. In reality, sickness and poor health may result in a loss of income, which is the main reason why people fall behind with their mortgage payments.

Social groups most at risk of mortgage indebtedness

It is believed that some social groups are more at risk than others from not being able to pay their mortgage payments (Nettleton and Burrows, 1998, p. 736). They include:

1   Households with younger children
2   Households with dependent children, especially lone parents
3   Single males
4   Divorced and separated
5   Economically inactive
6   Lower social classes
7   Employees in private sector at greater risk than those in public sector
8   Households from ethnic minorities

Indeed, it is argued that homeowners who are successful tend to be those who have higher incomes, educational levels, occupational status, and are older and married with children (Rohe and Van Zandt, p. 7).

Consequences of falling behind with mortgage payments

Failure to pay your mortgage has two grave consequences:

a)   your lender seeks to repossess your property
b)   your credit score will be affected by the mortgage arrears. This will affect your ability to apply for credit. All missed, late or partial payments are recorded on your credit file for at least six years.

However, according to Experian, its impact on your score will reduce as time passes, because lenders usually pay more attention to your most recent credit history. As long as you keep up with future payments, you should see your score improve over time, making it easier to get approved for credit at better rates.

If there is a good reason why you were late with a payment, such as redundancy, Experian's advice is to write and explain it to the lender concerned and get them to ask Experian to add a notice of correction to your report. This can be up to 200 words (Experian).

When a mortgage payment is late, it is best to contact your mortgage provider. If not, they will contact you to find out why your payment has not come through. At this point, they should give you the opportunity to get your payments back on track and will:

- tell you the total sum of your arrears
- list all the payments which you have missed
- tell you the exact amount outstanding under your mortgage
- give you a reasonable time to make good any shortfall in payments
- tell you the amount of any charges incurred because of missing any payments

Furthermore, your lender must not seek repossession unless all other reasonable attempts to resolve the situation have failed, and they must give you reasonable notice before taking that action (Money Advice Service).

Options when faced with difficulties paying mortgage

To help you with your difficulties meeting monthly mortgage payments, your lender may discuss with you several options:

Switch to an interest-only mortgage

Although this is not a long-term solution because you would only be repaying the interest part of the mortgage, it might provide temporary relief by reducing your monthly mortgage payment, assuming that you are on a repayment mortgage.

Extend the term of your mortgage

If you are on a repayment mortgage, extending the term reduces your monthly payments because you now have more time to repay your loan.

However, in the long term it will increase the overall cost of borrowing as more interest is charged.

If you are on an interest-only mortgage, extending the term makes no difference to your monthly payment as you only pay the interest on the mortgage, and not the capital.

Give you a payment holiday

This means you would have a break from paying your mortgage for a few months. You would need to catch up with these payments before your mortgage term ends. It is possible that your lender will still charge interest in this period, which would mean you would pay back more overall.

Help you with an assisted voluntary sale scheme

Your lender may offer an assisted voluntary sale scheme. This means they will give you extra time and help if you decide to sell your property.

Recommend government mortgage help

In some cases, you can get help from the government with your mortgage payments. This is called Support for Mortgage Interest (SMI). SMI is a **loan**, which you'll need to repay with **interest** when you sell or transfer ownership of your property.

However, it is worthwhile to note five key features of SMI:

1 It is designed to help with interest payments for a mortgage, for a loan to buy and to improve your home. It cannot be used to pay the amount you borrowed (i.e. the capital amount), insurance policies and mortgage arrears.
2 A homeowner may be eligible for SMI if they receive benefits such as income support, Jobseeker's Allowance, Employment and Support Allowance (ESA) and Universal Credit. However, there is a 39-week waiting period from the time you claim SMI until your first payment is made (unless you're getting Pension Credit, in which case you can get help immediately).
3 You can get help to pay interest on a loan or mortgage of up to £200,000.

4   SMI is normally paid direct to the lender (Gov.UK).
5   If you're claiming Jobseekers Allowance, you can only get SMI for up to two years. If you get Income Support, Income-related Employment and Support Allowance, Universal Credit or Pension Credit, there's no limit to how long you can claim SMI for (Money Advice Service, 'What is Support for Mortgage Interest?').

Repossession

Although many of us fear our homes being repossessed, this is always an act in the last resort. This can occur if you ignore the problem and do not contact or maintain a dialogue with your lender. In seeking repossession, a lender must follow five steps (Shelter).

Lender contacts you about mortgage arrears

Your lender will contact you if you miss a mortgage payment. They will ask you how you plan to pay back any arrears.

You can take steps to deal with mortgage arrears by:

* looking at your income and outgoings
* prioritising your debts
* preparing a financial statement

To help see where you can save money, you need to have a look at your outgoings in relation to what you have coming in then divide spending into essential and non-essential items.

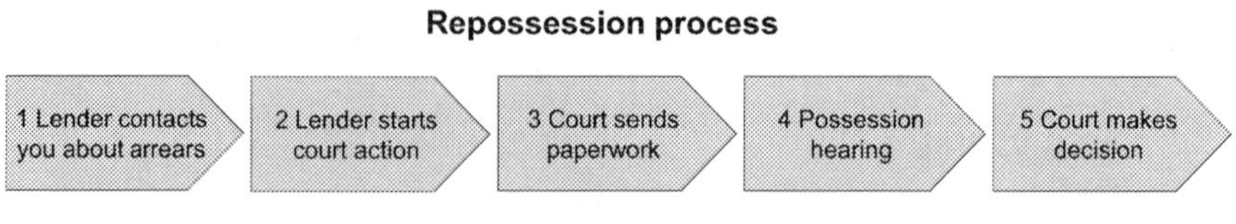

Repossession process

1 Lender contacts you about arrears → 2 Lender starts court action → 3 Court sends paperwork → 4 Possession hearing → 5 Court makes decision

Figure 9.1 Repossession process

CUTTING BACK SPENDING ON NON-ESSENTIALS

Budgeting is essential if you're struggling to meet outgoings. Here are just a couple of ways to cut back:

- **Look at the Direct Debits that go out of your account each month** – things like gym membership and magazine subscriptions. Now think about whether you are getting value for money out of all of them. If not, you may want to cancel them.
- **Try listing the smaller non-essential items you buy each day** – take-away coffees or drinks and other non-essentials can add up to a significant amount. You might want to list them all and put them in order of priority. Pick off the lower priority items first and cut them out one at a time.

CUTTING BACK SPENDING ON ESSENTIALS

Mortgage costs: Mortgage payments are often the largest monthly expenditure and so it is worthwhile to review your cost. You can speak to a mortgage adviser to find out if you can move to a cheaper deal.

Food and utilities: For things like food and energy bills – maybe you can try to save costs by shopping around to get a better deal elsewhere. Buying food at a cheaper supermarket can help you save, but you also need to budget to avoid over-spending.

Insurance: Insurance, especially life insurance and income protection, is essential if you do not have a large emergency fund. Therefore, think carefully before cancelling insurance premiums.

FIND WAYS TO INCREASE INCOME

Besides reducing expenses, you can also seek to find ways to increase your income. This could involve working overtime or selling unwanted items on eBay and Amazon.

SPEAK TO DEBT ADVICE ORGANISATIONS

A trained money adviser from an independent agency, like Citizens Advice or Shelter, can give you free and impartial advice. There are other charities that can help you talk through your situation and provide information on where to find solutions (Money Advice Service, 'Mortgage arrears').

You may be able to agree an affordable repayment plan with your lender. Alternatively, you might decide that your mortgage is unaffordable and ask the lender for time to sell your home.

Lender starts court action

It is in the interest of the lender to get you to pay the money you owe rather than repossess your property. If you are in mortgage arrears, your mortgage lender will want you to clear them. If you do not do this or cannot agree an action plan, your mortgage lender will start court action. This is called possession action and allows them to sell your home and use the money from the sale to recover the money you owe.

Most lenders do not want to repossess if they do not have to and will only use repossession as a last resort. After all, repossession is a lengthy and expensive process, with no guaranteed outcome. So, most lenders will not even consider it as an option until you have missed three months' worth of payments.

Mortgage lenders have to follow what is known as The Pre-Action Protocol for Mortgage Arrears. This protocol requires that you are properly and fully notified and given a chance to put things right before the repossession process is started. Most lenders issue a series of standard letters, typically with a 15-day deadline to respond. They must provide you with a list of all missed payments, the total level of arrears and the outstanding mortgage debt before they apply to court.

Eventually, you will be told that unless the arrears are paid, your lender will apply to a county court for an order to repossess your home. Your lender has to give you at least two weeks' notice in writing before they apply to the court.

The court sends you paperwork

If your lender starts court action, you will get a claim for possession of property from the county court. This will give you details about a court hearing and full details about the case against you.

As well as the claim for possession from the county court, you should also get a notice from your lender saying that court action has been started. The notice will not have your name on it and will be addressed to 'the tenant or the occupiers'.

The particulars of the claim will set out how much you owe your mortgage lender, how much you should be paying and what steps the lender has taken to collect the arrears. If there is any wrong or missing information on this form, you should tell the judge at the hearing (Citizens Advice).

THE DEFENCE FORM

Along with the claim form, there will be a defence form. You can use this to tell the court about your financial and personal circumstances and what attempts you have made to deal with the arrears. There is also a list of the money coming in and out of your household for you to complete. This is designed to help the judge decide how much you can afford to pay towards your arrears.

If you think you are not legally responsible for paying the mortgage, or you disagree with anything the lender has said in the particulars of the claim, you should use the defence form to say why. Other defensive claims in the form may include:

- you were pressurized by your partner into signing the mortgage agreement
- you think your lender has treated you unfairly or unreasonably
- you think your lender has not followed the procedures under *the pre-action protocol*

It is not a defence to say you cannot afford to pay the mortgage.

You should send the defence form back to the court before the hearing if possible, but you can also take it along on the day. If the lender has completed an online claim, you can send your defence to the court using the Possession Claim Online service.

The paperwork from the court also tells you:

- date, time and place of the hearing
- details about your mortgage and missed payments

You have three to eight weeks from when you get the paperwork until the hearing, and so use this time to prepare for the hearing.

You attend the possession hearing

It is essential that you attend the hearing even if the lender tells you that you do not need to. If you do not go, the court might grant an outright possession order which means you could be evicted from your home.

There are certain things you can do to prepare for the court hearing. Firstly, you need to think about the information the court might need, including:

- The defence form if you haven't already sent this in
- A financial statement. This has information about money you have coming in and going out of your household. You can use it to prove you can afford any offer you make to repay your arrears
- Any letters between you and the lender showing how you have tried to negotiate payment of your mortgage arrears
- If you're selling your property to pay off the arrears, your estate agent's details
- Proof of any payments you've made since the claim for possession of property was issued
- Proof of any claims you've made for state benefits or tax credits which you're still waiting to hear about
- Written confirmation of any lump sum payments you're waiting for, such as money you're owed in a will or for work that you've done for someone
- Proof of any payments under a mortgage payment protection insurance policy which you are due.

Secondly, you may find it helpful to note down the things you want to say to the judge when you get to court (Citizens Advice, 'How to prepare for court hearing').

The court makes a decision

The judge will carry out the hearing in the way they think will be fair to both sides.

If you don't have a legal adviser with you, the judge will usually give you help with how to handle the procedure of the hearing and the kind of evidence you can give.

Your mortgage lender or the person acting for them usually speaks first. You may find it helpful to take notes of anything they say that you disagree with.

The judge will want to be sure that both sides have followed the Mortgage Arrears Pre-Action Protocol. These are procedures you and your mortgage lender are expected to follow before the case comes to court.

The judge will also want to avoid granting your mortgage lender a possession order, as this could lead to you being evicted from your home.

You will be given the opportunity to argue why your home should not be repossessed and suggest solutions such as a repayment plan.

There are several possible outcomes:

a) A **suspended possession order** allows you to stay in your home on the terms set by the court. You have to pay a set amount on top of your normal monthly mortgage payment.

b) **An outright order**: is very serious, as it sets a date for you to leave your home. This could be as soon as four weeks after the hearing.

c) Other possible outcomes could include

- being ordered to pay the money you owe but without a repossession.
- You might be ordered to pay only part of what you owe or be given more time to pay.
- It also might be possible to request an adjournment to a later date, to give you more time to come up with a solution.
- You could even ask for the case to be thrown out if, for example, you feel your lender has not followed the correct protocols or has treated you unfairly (Property Investments UK).

When bailiffs can be asked to evict you

Even if your lender has successfully obtained an outright possession order, it does not mean you will be evicted immediately.

A Repossession Order and an Eviction Order (more correctly called a Warrant of Possession) are different.

The law states that the court must normally allow 28 days before a possession order comes into force and that this time period can be extended up to 56 days.

If you have not moved out in this time, then the lender can apply for a Warrant of Possession meaning that a bailiff can be brought in to evict you. All this can take several weeks.

Your lender can ask bailiffs to carry out an eviction if the court has made:

* an outright order and the date for possession has passed
* a suspended order and you break the terms of the order

Your lender must apply for an eviction warrant from the court. They must send a notice to your home to say they've done this. You could be evicted 14 days after this notice, unless you take action.

Sale of your home by the lender

If an eviction takes place, the mortgage lender will sell your home.

After the sale, the lender and any other secured creditors get their money and you receive anything left over.

You may have to pay off any mortgage shortfall to the lender if what you owe is more than the amount the property sells for.

Thus, the repossession process is lengthy and the outcome uncertain and so many lenders would want to avoid this. According to the 2015 repossession stats by Gov.UK, it takes:

* Approximately 20 weeks (five months) for the court to issue an order once a repossession claim is made by a mortgage company or lender.
* Between 80 and 90 weeks (20 months approximately) for the court to issue a warrant after a repossession order is issued.
* 100 weeks (nearly two years) or more for the actual repossession to complete from the day the claim was made (TIC Finance).

The lengthy repossession proceedings can cause a lot of stress and take a heavy toll on mental health. In 2014, a borrower sought compensation of £50,000 for financial loss and the stress and anxiety the enforcement action had caused them (MBM Commercial, 2016).

Arrears and repossessions

The proportion of possession claims ends up in repossessions varies between 30 and 50 per cent. In 2015, for example, 51 per cent of possession claims issued ended up in repossession, while in 2019 only 31 per cent of the claims issued resulted in repossession.

Table 9.3 Claims and repossessions in UK, 2015–19

Year	Claims issued	Orders – outright	Orders- suspended	Total	Warrants	Repossessions by county court bailiffs (England & Wales)	Properties taken into possession in UK
2015	19,852	7,984 (40%)	6,031 (30%)	14,015	23,220	5,592	10,220 (51%)
2016	18,456	7,274 (39%)	4,481 (24%0	11,755	17,627	4,754	7,700 (41.7%)
2017	19,836	8,270 (41.7%)	4,710 (23.7%)	12,980	16,336	4,386	7,330 (37%)
2018	19,508	8,093 (41.5%)	4,481 (23%)	12,574	15,772	4,126	6,750 (34.6%)
2019	25,580	10,575 (41.3%)	6,333 (24.7%)	16,908	18,142	4,929	7,920 (31%)

Source: Building Societies Association (n.d.)

The reason for the low number being repossessed is due to the reluctance of the courts to execute repossession orders, as repossession affects children and other dependants. In a study of the Irish mortgage market, it was found that many cases are stuck in the courts system, and they're being sent round and around waiting for adjournments.

Many mortgage holders are caught in a legal limbo, as county registrars, who handle civil bills for repossession, seek to mediate between borrowers and lenders. Their aim is to find a way to set up a payment arrangement that would satisfy the lender. One lender said that it takes between 18 and 72 months to repossess a home in Ireland, compared with 9–12 months in the UK, and six months in Northern Ireland and Denmark (Horgan-Jones, 2019).

Insuring the property

When you have a mortgage, the lender expects you to insure your property to protect their security from damage (e.g. fire). You therefore need to have buildings insurance in place at all times. If you have a leasehold property, the buildings insurance is normally included in the monthly service charge/cost. If you own a freehold property, then the responsibility to insure lies with you, the owner.

Some insurance companies can offer an unlimited rebuild cost, or up to a certain limit. If the price is dependent on the amount, then you need to know the rebuild cost. When you apply for a mortgage, the valuer often states a rebuild value or reinstatement cost on there, that is, the cost to rebuild your property if damaged. You must make sure that your insurance will pay you at least the amount equivalent to the rebuild value/reinstatement cost.

General conditions relating to the property

When you apply for a mortgage on a property in which you live in, lenders often stipulate a range of conditions, including:

a) That you must use your property as your only or main home unless your lender agrees otherwise
b) You must keep your property in good repair and condition
c) You must carry out and complete any building or repair work if it is needed to keep your property in good repair
d) You must make any payments relating to your property on time (e.g. pay any ground rent, service charges or stamp duty tax on time)
e) You must keep to any obligations you have relating to your property (e.g. if the property is leasehold, you must keep to the terms of the lease. If you acquire property under a government scheme to help you buy, or any similar scheme, you must comply with the requirements of that scheme)

It is in your self-interest to keep the property in good repair and condition, otherwise this will affect your enjoyment and the value on resale.

Seeking permission

Lenders often insist on borrowers to seek permission for the following:

a) Sell your property, give your property away or transfer the ownership of your property
b) Give someone else security over your property (e.g. if you wish to borrow extra money and give the second lender a second charge over your property, you need to seek permission from lender who holds a first charge)
c) Let your property or change the terms of any tenancy agreement. If the lender allows you to let your property, you are expected to

comply with any statutory obligations relating to the tenancy agreement including the Tenancy Deposit Scheme

d) Give up possession of your property or give someone (e.g. a paying lodger) a right to occupy all or part of your property
e) Change how your property is used or apply to any planning authority for consent to change its use
f) Make any significant changes to your property that affect its structure or add to it (e.g. building a conservatory or a garage)
g) Deal with any claim for compensation for the loss
h) Apply for or get a grant to do with your property

This list seems daunting but, in reality, you do have the freedom to enjoy your property and carry out improvements to enhance it. You only need to seek permission from the lender if your actions affect their legal ownership, for example, by giving another lender a legal right over the property or allowing people to stay in your property as lodgers or tenants. The reason you need permission in these cases is that your lender needs to make sure that their legal rights are protected and that they can take the property back when you cannot pay your mortgage payments.

Summary

A mortgage comes with financial responsibilities. You are expected to repay interest and capital over the term of the mortgage. Failure to do so means that the lender can take actions to take back the property, and you can be made homeless. Repossession is a lengthy process, creating a lot of uncertainty and stress for borrowers, and so it is best avoided.

The best way to ensure that you can meet your mortgage obligations is plan your future, embrace financial discipline and adopt three simple steps:

1 Set up an emergency fund to meet at least three to six months of expenses to enable you to pay any unexpected expenses and cope with a temporary fall in income.
2 Put in place an income protection policy to ensure you have a replacement income if you are unable to work.
3 Always live within your means and save 10–15 per cent of your income.

By following these simple steps, you will have the confidence to meet financial commitments, live with peace of mind, enjoy living in your property and avoid a precarious lifestyle.

[1] Deed is a written legal document which confirms the interest of a lender in the property. Few lenders now hold the deed due to the cost and risk of storage, and so many simply register a charge on the property with the Land Registry.

References

Building Societies Association, n.d., *Mortgage Arrears and Possessions.* Available at www.bsa.org.uk/statistics/mortgages-housing/mortgage-arrears-and-possessions.

Cadle, A., 2018, *Mortgage Arrears Biggest Source of Debt in Households Across UK*, 3 January 2018. Available at https://moneyage.co.uk/Mortgage-arrears-biggest-source-of-debt-in-households-across-UK.php#:~:text=Mortgage%20arrears%20are%20the%20biggest,a%20total%20of%20%C2%A33%2C581.

Cairney, J., and Boyle, M., 2004, 'Homeownership, Mortgages and Psychological Distress', *Housing Studies*, 19(2), pp. 161–174.

Citizens Advice, *What Happens When Your Mortgage Lender Takes You to Court.* Available at www.citizensadvice.org.uk/debt-and-money/mortgage-problems/what-happens-when-your-mortgage-lender-takes-you-to-court/.

Citizens Advice, *Your Mortgage Lender Takes You to Court – How to Prepare for the Court Hearing.* Available at www.citizensadvice.org.uk/debt-and-money/mortgage-problems/your-mortgage-lender-takes-you-to-court-how-to-prepare-for-the-court-hearing/.

Experian, *Late Payments and Your Credit Score.* Available at www.experian.co.uk/consumer/guides/late-payments.html [Accessed 7 May 2021].

FCA, *Mortgage Lending Statistics, Sept 2020.* Available at www.fca.org.uk/data/mortgage-lending-statistics.

Gov.UK, *Support for Mortgage Interest (SMI).* Available at www.gov.uk/support-for-mortgage-interest.

Horgan-Jones, J., 2019, *Life with Mortgage Arrears in Ireland: I Had 'Seizures from Stress.* Available at www.irishtimes.com/life-and-style/homes-and-property/life-with-mortgage-arrears-in-ireland-i-had-seizures-from-stress-1.3777654.

MBM Commercial, 2016, *Mortgage Repossession – Borrowers May Be Able to Claim Compensation Where Lenders Try to Enforce a Court Order Obtained Before a Change in the Law.* Available at https://mbmcommercial.co.uk/Latest-Blogs/Blogs/Mortgage-repossession.html.

Money Advice Service, *Mortgage Arrears or Problems Paying Your Mortgage.* Available at www.moneyadviceservice.org.uk/en/articles/mortgage-arrears-if-you-have-problems-paying-your-mortgage.

Money Advice Service, *What Is Support for Mortgage Interest.* Available at www.moneyadviceservice.org.uk/en/articles/support-for-mortgage-interest#how-long-can-you-get-smi-for.

The Money Charity, *Money Statistics: March 2020* [online]. Available at https:// themoneycharity.org.uk/money-statistics/.

Nettleton, S., and Burrows, R., 1998, 'Mortgage Debt, Insecure Home Ownership and Health: An Exploratory Analysis', *Sociology of Health & Illness*, 20(5), p. 735. Available at https://onlinelibrary.wiley.com/doi/ pdf/10.1111/1467-9566.00127.

Property Investments UK, *How Long Does It Take Before a House Is Repossessed Due to Mortgage Arrears?* Available at www.propertyinvestmentsuk.co.uk/ mortgage-arrears/.

Rohe, W., Van Zandt, S., and McCarthy, G., 2001, 'The Social Benefits and Costs of Homeownership: A Critical Assessment of the Research', *Joint Center for Housing Studies Harvard University*. Available at www.jchs.harvard.edu/sites/default/files/liho01-12.pdf.

Shelter, *Home Repossession Process*. Available at https://england.shelter.org.uk/ housing_advice/repossession/seven_steps_to_home_repossession.

Step Change, *Mortgage Arrears. What to Do If You're Struggling with Repayments*. Available at www.stepchange.org/debt-info/mortgage-arrears.aspx.

TIC Finance, *How Many Repossessions Year by Year: UK Repossessions Data 1969–2019*. Available at www.ticfinance.co.uk/stats/.

UK Finance, *Arrears and Repossessions*, 13 August 2020. Available at www. ukfinance.org.uk/data-and-research/data/mortgages/arrears-and-possessions#:~:text=Key%20data%20highlights%3A&text=There%20 were%2073%2C580%20homeowner%20mortgages,quarter%20of%20 the%20previous%20year.

Chapter Ten
How to protect your assets

If I had my way, I would write the word 'insure' upon the door of every cottage and upon the blotting book of every public man, because I am convinced, for sacrifices so small, families and estates can be protected against catastrophes which would otherwise smash them up forever.

It is the duty to arrest the ghastly waste, not merely of human happiness, but national health and strength, which follows when, through the death of the breadwinner, the frail boat in which the family are embarked, founders and the women and children and the estates are left to struggle in the dark waters of a friendless world.

Winston Churchill

A mortgage is often seen as a big burden because it involves keeping up with a financial commitment over a large part of our working life, commonly 25 years or more. Furthermore, mortgages are built on the assumption that borrowers have stable employment and good health over a long period of time, allowing them to receive an undisrupted flow of income to meet mortgage payments.

Yet, life is full of uncertainties, with everyone faces a daunting prospect of unexpected death, poor health and redundancy, resulting in a loss of income. Indeed, a loss of income is one of the main causes of mortgage difficulties.

The good news is that you can do something to ensure that life uncertainties do not affect your ability to pay your mortgage and keep your home. There are three possible strategies for you to protect yourself: (1) build a financial buffer, (2) reduce the risk and (3) transfer the risk to an insurance company. This chapter examines the risks you face and what you can do to mitigate them, so that you can avoid mortgage payment difficulties and the risk of losing your home.

Factors affecting mortgage payments and strategies to reduce risks of mortgage difficulties

In Chapter 9, we have looked at three types of factors (structural, household and expenditure, and personal) that cause people to have difficulties meeting their mortgage payments. These factors are summarised below, along with ways to mitigate against them.

Structural factors

One great risk that reduces a household's ability to pay its mortgage is a sudden rise of mortgage interest rate to an unaffordable level. In the

Table 10.1 Factors affecting ability to pay mortgage payments and possible solutions

Types of factors	Factors	Ways to tackle
Structural factors	Interest rate changes	Fix mortgage rate
	Loan-to-value ratio causing negative equity	Buy in desirable and popular areas to reduce risk of falling demand and house price, and put down a bigger deposit where possible
	Income to loan ratio	Ensure mortgage payments are affordable and not above 30% of income
Household and expenditure factors	Unemployment	Transfer the risk
	Sickness/poor health	Transfer the risk
	Death	Transfer the risk
	Unanticipated repairs	Transfer the risk or self-insure
	Short-term working	Savings/emergency fund
Personal factors	Money management skills	Learn to budget, save 10%–15% of income, avoid over-spending, pay off mortgage quickly
	Commitment to pay mortgage debt	

Source: Adapted from Nettleton and Burrows (1998)

Table 10.2 Interest rates in UK, 1980–2020

Periods	Bank base rate
1980–89	8.4%–14.88%
1990–99	5.5%–13.88%
2000–08	2%–6%
2009–19	0.25–0.75%
2020	0.1%

Source: NGI Residential, 'Rise and fall: historical interest rates in UK, 1979–2019'

1980s, for example, bank base rates were high, reaching 14.88 per cent in 1989. As a result, mortgage rates rose from an interest rate of 9.8 per cent in April 1988 to 15.4 per cent in 1990. Bank base rates began to fall after 1992. After the financial crisis in 2009, the Bank of England base rate fell to 0.5 per cent, and stayed at this rate for many years. In March 2020, due to the COVID-19 pandemic, the bank base rate fell further to 0.1 per cent.

Changes in interest rate will cause a change in income-to-loan ratio. A fall in interest rate means that your monthly mortgage payment might form a smaller proportion of a household income, while a rise means that it might comprise a bigger proportion.

Financial planners suggest that all monthly household debt payments should not make up more than 40 per cent of the total monthly gross income. Ideally, the ratio should be 0.36 (or 36%) or less. Housing costs normally consume a significant proportion of a household's income but it is recommended that the total cost (mortgage payments, taxes and insurance) should not constitute more than 25 to 29 per cent of gross annual income (Garman & Forgue, 2018, p. 275; Madura, 2014, p. 266).

To help borrowers manage their household budget, lenders started to introduce fixed-rate mortgages since 1990. In his review of the mortgage market (12 March 2004), Professor David Miles of Imperial College London argued that borrowers could protect themselves from the negative effects of an interest rate increase by fixing one of their main monthly household expenses. This certainty of payment would also give them peace of mind (Jarvis, 2005).

In the same year, the Chancellor Gordon Brown commissioned Professor Miles to examine why long-term fixed-rate mortgages were less common in the UK than they were in the US and continental Europe. In the UK, most fixed-rate mortgages lasted between two and five years, while US homebuyers could choose from 10-, 15-, 20- and 30-year terms, and in Germany, Austria and Sweden, between 10 and 25 years. The research concluded that the funding of mortgages in the UK was different from other countries, and that there was a low desire among consumers to choose certainty over price. In 2005, fixed-rate mortgages made up around 35 per cent of the new mortgage lending market, below their peak of 50 per cent in 1999 (Jarvis, 2005).

Long-term fixed-rate mortgages have become more popular. An analysis by the Bank of England shows that long-term fixed-rate mortgages have become more popular since 2016, with five years or longer fixed-rate mortgages accounting for more half of the mortgages issued in 2019 Q4. The Bank of England believes that low interest rates have made long-term fixed-rate mortgages attractive (Bank of England, 2020). Indeed, one bank (Habito) has launched a 40-year fixed-rate mortgage in the UK (Osborne, 2021).

A second risk when you buy a property is a change in loan-to-value ratio. This happens when house prices fall and the value of your mortgage becomes higher than the value of the house. For example, you buy a property for £100,000 and borrow a mortgage of £90,000 (90 per cent of the value). If the value of the house goes up to £110,000 (10 per cent increase), you have a £20,000 equity (10 per cent from your deposit and 10 per cent from the rise in price).

If the value of the house falls by 10 per cent to £90,000, you have no equity and lose your 10 per cent deposit if you sell the property.

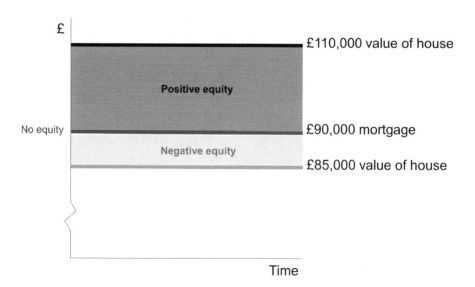

Figure 10.1 Negative equity

However, if the property price falls by 15 per cent to £85,000, you have a negative equity because the value of the house is now worth £5,000 less than the mortgage. If you sell the property, you will lose your deposit and have to find an additional £5,000 to pay the lender because the sale price (£85,000) is inadequate to repay a £90,000 mortgage. Buyers who put down a small deposit face the highest risk of falling into negative equity if property prices fall. One solution is to wait for the house price to rise before selling the property.

Household and expenditure factors

Changes in household and expenditure factors, such as a sudden fall or loss of income or an unexpected increase in expenses, can also cause difficulties in paying mortgage payments. The most serious factors causing changes in income levels are pre-mature death, poor health and unemployment which can result in a reduction or total loss of income. These can have a prolonged adverse impact and so it is recommended to transfer the risk to an insurance company. This will be discussed more fully below.

A household can also face an unexpected rise in expenses due to unanticipated and expensive repairs (e.g. boiler or car breakdown). Some of these risks can be managed by taking out an appropriate insurance policy. For example, a boiler breakdown can be expensive to repair so you may want to consider taking out a boiler cover which pays for any repairs in the event of a breakdown. However, not all repairs are insurable (e.g. car repairs) and therefore you need to have savings to pay for these when they arise.

Components of personal wealth

Personal wealth comprises three elements: human capital, property and financial. Human capital is the most important aspect of wealth because it generates income to pay for mortgage payments and to save and invest for the future. Human capital and property are insurable, but financial wealth is not. In the following sections, we will discuss why it is important to insure your human capital and your property.

Human capital and risks of loss

The loss of human capital is likely to have the greatest impact on a household income, and therefore its ability to meet financial commitments. In simple

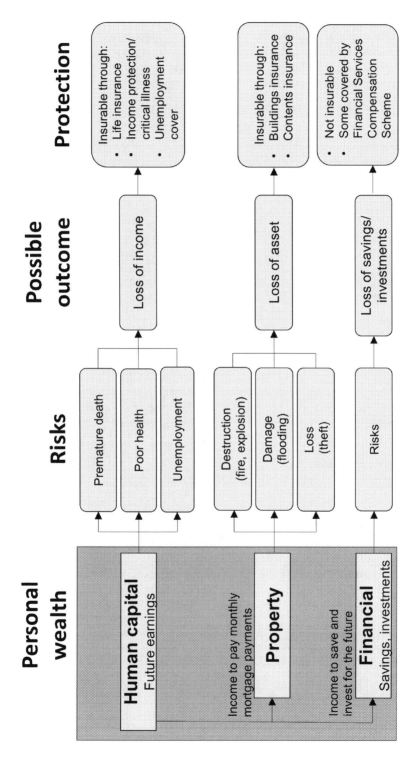

Figure 10.2 Components of personal wealth and insurance

terms, human capital can be defined as the amount of income we receive over our lifetime from our skills, experience, knowledge, and qualifications.

Human capital is our largest and most important asset in the early years of our working life when we have limited financial assets. The younger we are, the more reliant we are on our human capital. For most people under 30, human capital is believed to account for 90 per cent of total assets or wealth they possess. Even for those in their 50s, it is thought that human capital still represents at least half of their total wealth (Johnson and Horan, 2013).

A major disadvantage of human capital is that, unlike financial or property assets, it is not tangible, visible or liquid. We cannot cash in the value of our human capital when we need the money nor can we sell it. We cannot have all the value of our human capital now, but have to be patient and slowly convert it into a monetary value. In fact, we need time, good health and demand for our skills to turn human capital into money or financial wealth.

Human capital is fragile and subjected to three main risks: pre-mature death, poor health and unemployment. These events lead to a loss of income, preventing us from meeting our mortgage obligations.

In the face of these risks, we can ignore, reduce or eliminate them. Ignoring these risks can have devastating financial consequences and so the real choice is between risk reduction/elimination and self-insurance. In the following sections, we will discuss three main risks and how you can mitigate against them.

The risk of dying young

The greatest risk we all face is dying young, also known as premature death. Although statistically the probability of dying young is low (1 per cent), the financial impact of death is devastating because it results in the total loss of human capital and associated future earnings. Death can lead to the loss of the family home, create real financial hardship for surviving family members, and can push families into poverty.

The impact of premature death

LOSING YOUR HOME

One of the most pressing financial issues immediately after the death of a breadwinner is whether their family and surviving dependants are safe

Table 10.3 Impact of death on homeowners and renters

Types of home owners	Impact of death
Home owners with no mortgage or have paid off	Feel confident there would not be immediate financial issues relating to housing costs and they could stay in their home
Home owners with life insurance	Face some element of uncertainty as administration takes time while current mortgage liabilities continue
	Financial uncertainty causes anxiety, and lengthy administrative process means emotional strain and practical problems in trying to meet mortgage payments until things are settled.
	Takes 3–4 months before mortgages are paid off through life insurance
	People who cannot meet mortgage payments during these transitions have to borrow money
	Uncertainties are eventually resolved
Home owners with no protection	High uncertainties and financial problems about accommodation
	Face distress, debt and anxiety
	Have to make hard decisions: sell, move in with relatives or a quick sale at a reduced price at a time of emotional distress

Source: Corden et al. (2008, pp. 106–108)

in their home. Many attach deep emotional significance to the property and most want to stay on. After the death of a breadwinner, many may not have a choice and their future is dependent on whether the mortgage has been paid off or not, and whether there is life insurance in place to pay off the mortgage (Corden et al., 2008).

Research shows that those who have paid off their mortgage feel confident that they have no financial problems with housing costs and they could stay in their home. Those who have a mortgage face an uncertain future.

Homeowners with a life insurance policy may face short-term cash-flow issues, as it might take time (3–4 months) for a life insurance policy to be processed. Placing a life insurance policy in a trust helps speed up the process as the proceeds are paid direct to the beneficiaries, rather than to the deceased person's estate.

Homeowners with a mortgage but have no life insurance policy in place face a bleak future. During times of great emotional distress, they have to make a hard decision of whether to sell their home, move in with relatives or go for a quick sale by agreeing to sell their property below its true value (20–30 per cent).

Seen from this perspective, repaying a mortgage early also gives survivors peace of mind and security in the event of death of a breadwinner. If this is not possible, then a mortgage needs to be protected, and a life insurance policy should be placed in a trust to avoid delays.

UNEXPECTED EXPENSES

While losing an income, death creates additional expenses, such as funeral, probate (confirmation in Scotland) and estate settlement costs, and inheritance taxes for larger estates, and these have to be paid quickly.

In 2020, the average cost of a burial was £5,000 and cremation £4,000. However, there are also send-off costs (such as flowers, a memorial, catering, limo hire, venue hire, flowers, order sheets/service cards, funeral and death notice) totalling around £2,300 and professional fees (£2,800) to consider (SunLife, 2020). In other words, the total cost of death is approximately £10,000.

In the face of these costs, some people have to borrow money on a credit card, from friends and relatives and banks, or sell possessions to raise money to pay for funeral costs. The surge in funeral costs has resulted in 'debt poverty' as families who struggle with funeral costs take on debt. In 2019, the average debt taken on by bereaved families who struggled to pay was £1,990 (Royal London, 2019).

STRESS

Survivors face additional stress as they may have to take on new roles within the family and domestic life: greater responsibilities for child care, household management, shopping and cooking, money management and driving. Taking on these new roles is often stressful, leading to increased anxieties, frustrations and disappointments (Corden et al., 2008).

How can you protect your family against the financial impact of death?

There are two ways to alleviate the financial impact of death on your family: accumulate savings (self-insure) or transfer the risk to a life insurance company.

A life insurance policy is highly recommended because survivors have an immediate access to a capital value (i.e. the sum assured) from day one. For example, if you take out a life insurance policy of £200,000, your survivors will be paid £200,000 from the day the policy starts. Savings, on other hand, take years to build up.

For a high amount, life assurance policy is clearly better than savings which require a long time to build up the required savings/capital, and exposes individuals to insufficient funds in the meantime (Mahdzan and Diacon, 2008).

LIFE INSURANCE

Life insurance has been described as 'money to deal with death's financial fallout'. It is designed to provide survivors with a lump sum to pay off debts and funeral expenses, and a replacement income. It can play a powerful role in the transitionary life for survivors, by providing the necessary financial resources to enable them to avoid money worries, take time off work and focus on grieving (Lynch, 2009).

In the UK, there are three main types of life insurance – lump sum term assurance, whole of life and family income benefit.

TERM ASSURANCE

A lump sum term assurance contract is relatively cheap because it provides coverage for a limited period, normally set up to age 65, and a single lump sum amount is paid only if death occurs in this period.

Term insurance provides pure insurance coverage because nothing is paid if you do not die during the term of your life insurance policy. In the UK, many policies are set to expire at age 65 but on average people live to the age of 80. This means that few term life insurance policies are paid out, and thus the cost is relatively low.

CONSIDERATIONS WHEN TAKING OUT A LIFE INSURANCE POLICY

Taking out a life insurance policy requires many decisions at the start of the policy, including who needs to be insured, how much cover, how long is the term, what type of policy (term insurance or whole of life insurance), should the policy be single or joint, and which insurance provider to choose.

Figure 10.3 How to calculate life insurance needs

Source: Author's diagram

The most important decision is deciding how much cover to buy and for how long. This will depend on several needs, as shown in Figure 10.3.

- **Capital needs**: this is the amount needed to pay off a mortgage and any other loans, emergency funds, specific legacies and any inheritance tax liability.
- **Short-term capital needs**: the amount required to pay for funeral expenses and other debts.
- **Income needs**: this is the amount of replacement income your survivors require to maintain their lifestyle.

A rough rule of thumb suggests that a working parent should insure a lump sum amount worth between five and ten times their annual salary to meet the family's income needs. For example, for someone with a salary of £20,000, a £200,000 life insurance is recommended.

In reality the amount of life insurance needed depends on the amount of borrowing outstanding and the living costs of the survivors, both of which can vary depending on where they live. As the biggest debt is usually a mortgage loan, those in London and the South East will probably need a higher amount of life insurance, due to higher property prices (thus mortgage) and funeral costs.

DEATH BENEFITS FROM YOUR EMPLOYER

The good news is that some of your needs may be met by benefits you get from work. Many employers in the UK provide life and health benefits to their employees. In 2019, 8.6 million people were members of group life schemes and thus were provided with death-in-service benefit (ABI, 2019). The amount of death in service is often given as a multiple of your salary (typically two to three times your salary).

However, this is tied to your employer and if you leave your employment, the benefit ceases.

The government also offers some benefits to support surviving husbands, wives and civil partners in the event of death in the form of bereavement benefits. Bereavement Support Payment consists of an initial lump sum payment of £2,500 (or, if you have children, £3,500) and a further 18 monthly instalments of £100 (or, if you're eligible for Child Benefit, £350).

As these payments are not sufficient to pay for funeral costs or living expenses, many people will need to take out additional private cover to ensure that their loved ones can maintain their living standards.

Whole of life policy

A whole of life policy is designed for those who have an inheritance tax liability. It is more expensive than term life insurance because it insures you for the whole of your life, and thus is guaranteed to pay out. The policy has no expiry date (but is renewable every 5–10 years), and the policy pays out a lump sum if death occurs.

There are two elements to the policy: investment and insurance. Part of the premium is used to invest, and the other part to fund the cost of providing life insurance. This means that if you cancel the policy, there is a value and you might get some money back. A term life assurance, on the other hand, has no cash-in value if the policy is cancelled and you do not get anything back, and this explains why it is more affordable. Term life insurance is therefore recommended for those who need protection but have a limited budget.

Family income benefit

While a term or a whole of life policy pays out a lump sum to enable survivors to pay off liabilities, they often have no income to live on and may be forced to live in relative poverty.

A family income benefit policy is therefore designed to provide a replacement income to ensure that survivors can maintain their standards of living when a breadwinner dies and a family loses its main source of income. This policy is more affordable than a whole of life and a term life policy because it only provides an income, and the policy benefit is decreasing. For example, a family takes out a family income benefit policy to provide £20,000 of income for 20 years. If a claim is made in year 1, a family receives payments for 20 years. If a claim is made in year 20, a family receives payments for one year. In other words, the number of years of payout is reduced as every year passes.

In summary, life insurance and family income benefit are used as complementary solutions to provide money to meet capital and income needs.

Risk of poor health

The risk of poor health – or more formally known as morbidity risk – is a far greater risk than the risk of premature death. The Health and Safety Executive (HES) reports that more than 1.6 million workers in the UK suffered from work-related ill health in 2019–20, caused by stress, depression or anxiety (51 per cent), musculoskeletal disorders (30 per cent) and other type of illness (19 per cent). As a result, 32.5 million working days were lost, costing more than £16 billions annually (HES, 2020).

These costs include financial costs (e.g. loss of output, healthcare costs and other payments made) and human costs (e.g. monetary valuation given to pain, grief, suffering and loss of life). Individuals bear nearly 60 per cent of these costs, with the remainder split between the government (21 per cent) and employers (20 per cent) (Health and Safety Executive, 2020). Mental health has also become a prominent issue, and 300,000 people with a long-term mental health problem lose their jobs each year (Farmer and Stevenson, 2017).

According to Aviva, more than 57 per cent of families would struggle if they lose a source of income permanently (Aviva, 2017). This is not surprising, as many households do not have an adequate safety net and their living standards will be affected if their household income drops. In 2018–19, 12.8 million households (46 per cent of the total) in the UK had either no savings or less than £1,500 in savings. In total, 19.2 million households (68 per cent of the total) had less than £10,000 in savings (The Money Charity, 2020).

Another report paints a bleaker picture. In 2020, 1 in 10 Brits (9 per cent) had no savings at all, a third less than £600 in savings, and 41 per cent did not have enough savings to live for a month without an income. The average person in the UK had £6,757 saved (Boyle, 2020), but they require a greater level of savings to feel secure.

Research by Legal and General shows that an average amount of household savings is £2,729, but many people say they need £12,200 of savings to make them feel financially secure for one year. However, the life insurer argues that, based on typical monthly outgoings, the required amount is £30,000 (Legal and General, Deadline to Breadline, 2020). For those with limited or no savings, it is important to have an insurance policy in place, as this can provide a replacement income in the event of ill health.

Help from the government and employers

In the UK, when people are off sick, there are some state benefits available. If an employee leaves work due to health or disability, employers are required to pay statutory sick pay (SSP) for up to 28 weeks (six months). Some employers (43 per cent) offer some form of sick pay over and above minimum statutory requirements in the form of occupational sick pay (OSP).

When SSP ends, an employee can then apply for state welfare benefits (employment and support allowance ESA) provided that they have paid National Insurance for at least two years. ESA is initially paid for 13 weeks during which applicants go through a work capability assessment to determine their eligibility.

Although there is some sick pay benefit provided in the UK, there are three fundamental issues.

Firstly, employees receive sick pay for a maximum period of 28 weeks (just over six months).

Secondly, the amount of payment is well below the average UK household weekly spending – in fact, the payment constitutes only 17 per cent of the average weekly spend (Smith, 2020). There is thus a big shortfall (83 per cent) between what you might need and what you receive.

Thirdly, when the SSP payment ends, eligibility to sick pay is means-tested and entitlement unclear.

The UK welfare system has been criticised because it assumes that households who get little or no support recognise this and put in place their own safety net (ABI, 2014). It is recommended that UK households should be given more information to enable them to have a clearer understanding of:

1   How much income support they can get from the state if they stop work due to ill health
2   How much income support they will get from their employer
3   How they can top up their income safety net to the level they need.

The self-employed in the UK fare a lot worse as they are not entitled to statutory sick pay. Though they can claim ESA, their eligibility is not guaranteed and this is means-tested.

How can you protect yourself and your family from poor health?

Sick pay from your employer and the government goes some way to help but you might need to take out a private policy to cater for your needs and your circumstances. For example, you might need a longer period of time to recover and a higher amount of income to meet your expenses. An individual policy can be tailored to meet your lifestyle needs.

There are three possible courses of action you can take to provide financial security for you and your family: (1) savings, (2) insurance policy or (3) alternative sources of income. The following section focuses on savings and transferring the risks.

Savings

Having an emergency fund is essential, because it provides a financial buffer to cope with the unexpected. Financial planners recommend that everyone should have an emergency fund equivalent to at least 3–6 months' salary or income, whichever is greater. Some people might need a bigger emergency fund, up to 12 months, depending on their circumstances.

Income protection policy

Many people in the UK are reliant on good health to be able to go to work and earn a living. If they fall ill and are unable to work, they would not receive an income. In order to maintain their standard of living and avoid poverty in the event of ill health, it is important to have a replacement income.

Income protection policy, also known as permanent health insurance, is designed to provide a replacement income when a policyholder is unable to work due to poor health. It covers a wide range of conditions, from progressive illness (cancer), mental illness or depression, musculoskeletal problems, heart, blood pressure or blood circulation problems, stomach, liver, kidney or digestive problems, chest or breathing problems to stress. In 2019, more than 27,000 income protection claims were paid, with musculoskeletal problems responsible for the highest number of claims, followed by mental health and then cancer (ABI, 2020).

An income protection policy can protect our income for the whole of our working life. Indeed, it can provide cover for more than 52 years, if the policy starts at age 18 and ends at age 70. Income protection insurance allows the insured to protect a large percentage of their income – up to 50–70 per cent – which is paid out tax-free. There is no limit on the number of claims you can make.

However, many people do not have a policy in the UK. In fact, Aviva calculates that only around 8 per cent of adults in the UK have an income protection policy (Aviva, 2017). The income protection gap is enormous. Swiss Re estimated that the income protection gap in the UK amounted to £175 billions of annual benefit in 2015. In 2017, this gap rose to an estimated £200 billion and the total estimated 'protection gap' in the UK was £2.4 trillion (Contractor Weekly, 2017).

The low uptake of income protection is partly due to a lack of awareness of the benefits. Aviva reports that 40 per cent of parents in the UK do not think they ever need or want income protection. Yet, income protection is the most important tool they have against long-term disability because it protects their income for the whole of their working life. If an individual cannot work due to ill health, an income protection policy provides a replacement income, allowing them to avoid a fall in living standards and poverty. Income protection has been aptly described as a wealth preservation tool, as in the event of long-term disability you will receive payments from an insurance company rather than deplete your savings.

However, an income protection policy may not offer a suitable solution for everyone. The policies are relatively expensive and have tight eligibility and claim criteria. The cost is determined by a wide range of factors, including age, occupation, smoker status, the length of term, benefit amount, deferred period (waiting period before a claim is made) and medical history. In addition, the level of cover and premium are determined at the start of the policy, and so if earnings are lower at the point of claim, an individual may pay more for a policy.

Critical illness cover

Income protection pays a monthly income to enable you to meet expenses. However, you might also need a lump sum to pay off debts, or pay for treatments (e.g. speech therapy) and adjustments to the home (e.g. wheelchair access). A critical illness policy is designed to pay a one-off lump sum.

A critical illness policy pays out on a diagnosis of a range of critical conditions (up to 40 or more conditions and some insurers cover over 100), such as cancer, stroke and heart attack. In 2019, according to the ABI, cancer was the biggest single reason for an individual critical illness claim.

A critical illness policy often requires a 14–30 days survival period – that is, an individual must survive this period for the insurance company to pay out. If they do not survive the minimum period, there is no payout. For this reason, a critical illness policy is often combined with life insurance, so that payment will be made on a diagnosis of a critical condition or death.

It is estimated that 9 per cent of individuals in the UK have a critical illness policy, in comparison to 12 per cent who have phone insurance. Yet, the risk of developing a critical illness is real. A male non-smoker aged 40, for example, is 4.1 times more likely to be diagnosed with a critical illness than die before retiring at 65 years old. There are 7.4 million people living with heart and circulatory diseases in the UK, and 2.5 million with cancer, estimated to increase to 4 million by 2030 (Smith, 2020).

A critical illness causes financial strains on individuals, as they may not be able to work full-time, if at all, while their expenses rise. They might have to spend more money on healthcare costs, buy new clothes due to weight loss/gain and pay more for heating (Smith, 2020). Indeed, Royal London reported that 3.5 million people who were diagnosed with a critical illness between 2012 and 2017 were not able to cope financially (Royal London, 2017). Having a critical illness policy can help alleviate financial stress in times of need.

Income protection and critical illness policies are complementary rather than alternatives, as one provides an income and the other a lump sum. Where budget is an issue, income protection is recommended because it covers more conditions (mental illness and back trouble) than critical illness and provides a regular income.

Mortgage payment protection insurance

Besides income protection and critical illness cover, those with financial commitments may also wish to consider mortgage payment protection insurance (MPPI). This policy will pay a set amount each month, normally for a period of up to two years. There are three different types of policies: unemployment only, accident and sickness only, or accident, sickness and unemployment (ASU). As an ASU policy is the most comprehensive, it is the most expensive.

A mortgage payment protection insurance policy offers two types of cover. First, you can have a policy covering the cost of your mortgage payments only, or the cost of other bills too. In the case of the latter, the policy will typically cover 125 per cent of your mortgage costs. Second, you can choose to base the cover on your salary, and can protect up to 50 per cent of your monthly salary (Which, 2021). While a MPPI policy provides protection against three causes of income loss (unemployment, accident, and sickness), it is only a short-term policy, giving cover for up to 24 months.

In summary, employers and the government offer various types of benefits to help you cope in the event of ill health. It is important to understand what these benefits are, how much they offer and how long these are paid. If these are not sufficient to allow you to maintain the lifestyle you have been accustomed to, it might be necessary to consider private provision.

Experts generally agree that income protection is probably the most important protection product to buy, because it gives you a source of income if you are unable to work in the event of disability or long-term illness. If you have low or no savings, an income protection policy is critical, while for those who have savings, an income protection policy can act as a wealth preservation tool.

Case study

The first five years of Mary's mortgage were uneventful. She bought her house with her partner in 2010. Despite the economic headwinds, both were working. With two children, they wanted a permanent place to call home.

But in 2015, her partner, who rides a motorbike for work, was in a serious accident, [which resulted] in multiple broken bones and seriously injuries.

Without sick pay, Mary – working part-time – was the only earner. The family quickly slipped into mortgage arrears. Then the phone calls from the bank started. Soon they were €10,000 in arrears.

The pressure was building. 'The bank was like "when will you pay, what are you paying, when will you clear the arrears?"'

The family fell behind on credit card payments, then electricity and gas bills – ultimately they ended up going to a neighbourhood loan shark to make ends meet. When Mary's family found out, they cleared the debt owed to the loan shark. But the 'dark times' continued after her family bailed her out.

'It compounded my depression more, because I felt like I was a big burden on my family', she says.

Source: Horgan-Jones (2019)

Personal factors

Changes to a household's level of income and expenses do not necessarily result in mortgage difficulties. What is decisive is how we respond to these changes.

Your attitude to a mortgage is critical and determines your actions and priorities. If you see a mortgage as a serious commitment that receives the highest priority, you need to be willing to make sacrifices to ensure your mortgage payments can be paid. This may involve personal sacrifices such as forgoing spending on entertainment, going out and having fun, or working extra hours to earn more money. Mortgage payments, after all, are priority debts, because failure to pay your mortgage payments could lead to the loss of your home.

You also need to use your money management skills to help you manage your financial commitments. There are three simple principles to follow to ensure that you can always meet your financial obligations:

1   Control expenditure through budgeting, so that you can avoid over-spending
2   Live within your means and avoid personal debt
3   Put aside at least 10–15 per cent of your income for the future

Using these principles, some people seek to repay their mortgage as quickly as possible to allow them to be mortgage free. Years ago, a couple bought a three-bed house, and rented out two rooms and used the money to overpay the mortgage. They also had no children and worked at weekends and evenings to earn extra money to overpay the mortgage. They managed to pay off the mortgage in a few years, instead of the usual 25-year timescale. This involved a lot of personal sacrifice and hard-work in the short term but it meant that they were able to enjoy a life without a mortgage early in life before the arrival of their children.

Embracing financial discipline, such as budgeting, putting aside 10–15 per cent of income and avoiding over-spending, reduces the risk of falling into financial difficulties, and ensures that you will always have a roof over your head.

Protecting your property

In addition to protecting an individual's ability to earn an income, the property itself needs protection from damage, destruction and theft through fire, flooding, terrorism by taking out a policy called building insurance.

Building insurance

Buildings insurance covers the full cost of rebuilding your house or repairing damage to the structure of your property. Garages, sheds and fences are also covered, as well as the cost of replacing items such as pipes, cables and drains, and the costs of demolition, site clearance and architects' fees.

Buildings insurance usually covers loss or damage caused by:

- fire, explosion, storms, floods, earthquakes
- theft, attempted theft and vandalism
- frozen and burst pipes
- fallen trees, lamp posts, aerials or satellite dishes
- subsidence
- vehicle or aircraft collisions

After September 11, terrorism insurance is offered by some insurers as an extra cost.

When you buy building insurance, insurers can offer you insurance based on an unlimited sum to rebuild or repair your property, or on the rebuild value of your property. The rebuild cost is stated in a valuation report prepared by a surveyor.

Contents insurance

Home contents insurance covers you against loss, theft or damage to your personal and home possessions. It can also cover you if you take items (e.g. jewellery, mobile phones) out of the home, on holiday, for example.

Summary

Taking on a mortgage requires you to think ahead and plan your future so that you can deal with the unexpected. This involves having an emergency fund (equivalent to 3–6 months of expenses as a minimum) to deal with short-term needs and taking out insurance policies to enable you to cope in the long term.

If you are young and single, an income protection is a must, as this provides a replacement income if you are unable to work due to poor health. If you have dependants and a mortgage, then life insurance and income protection are recommended, so that you and your loved ones are protected from the adverse financial impact of death and poor health.

References

ABI, 2014, *Welfare Reform for the 21st Century: The Role of Income Protection Insurance*, available at www.abi.org.uk/globalassets/sitecore/files/documents/publications/public/2014/protection/welfare-reform-for-the-21st-century.pdf [Accessed 30 April 2021].

ABI, 2019, *UK Insurance and Long-Term Savings: Key Facts*, December 2019, p. 23. Available at www.abi.org.uk/globalassets/files/publications/public/key-facts/key_facts_2019_spread.pdf [Accessed 23 November 2020].

ABI, 2020, 'Record 98.3% of protection claims paid out in 2019'. Available at https://www.abi.org.uk/news/news-articles/2020/05/record-98.3-of-protection-claims-paid-out-in-2019/.

Aviva, 2017, *Protecting Our Families Report March 2017*. Available www.aviva.com/newsroom/public-policy-items/protecting-our-families-report-march-2017 [Accessed 23 November 2020].

Bank of England, 2020, *Why Are More Borrowers Choosing Long-Term Fixed-Rate Mortgage Products* [online]. Available at https://www.bankofengland.co.uk/bank-overground/2020/why-are-more-borrowers-choosing-long-term-fixed-rate-mortgage-products [Accessed 30April 2021].

Boyle, M., 2020, 'Saving Statistics: Average Savings in the UK 2020', *Finder* [online]. Available at www.finder.com/uk/saving-statistics [Accessed 23 November 2020].

Contractor Weekly, 2017, *The UK's £2.4 Trillion Protection Gap* [online]. Available at www.contractorweekly.com/insurance-news/uks-2-4-trillion-protection-gap/ [Accessed 23 November 2020].

Corden, A., Hirst, M., and Nice, K., 2008, *Financial Implications of Death of a Partner*, Working Paper No. ESRC 2288 12.08. Available at www.york.ac.uk/inst/spru/research/pdf/Bereavement.pdf, p. 107 [Accessed 23 November 2020].

Farmer, P. and Stevenson, D., 2017, *Thriving at Work The Stevenson / Farmer Review of Mental Health and Employers* [online]. Available at https://assets.publishing.service.gov.uk/government/uploads/system/uploads/attachment_data/file/658145/thriving-at-work-stevenson-farmer-review.pdf. [Accessed 30 April 2021].

Garman, E.T. and Forgue, R.E., 2018, *Personal Finance* (13th edition, Cengage Learning, Boston).

Health and Safety Executive (HES), 2020, *Health and Safety at Work: Summary Statistics for Great Britain 2020* [online]. Available at https://www.hse.gov.uk/statistics/overall/hssh1920.pdf [Accessed 30 April 2021].

Horgan-Jones, J., 2019, 'Life With Mortgage Arrears in Ireland: I Had "Seizures from Stress"', *Irish Times*, 2 February 2019. Available at www.irishtimes.com/life-and-style/homes-and-property/life-with-mortgage-arrears-in-ireland-i-had-seizures-from-stress-1.3777654 [Accessed 30 April 2021].

Jarvis, A., 2005, '15-years Since the Peak of Mortgage Rates', *Mortgage Introducer*, 7 February 2005. Available at www.mortgageintroducer.com/15-years-since-the-peak-of-mortgage-rates/#:~:text=From%20an%20interest%20rate%20of,popularity%20of%20fixed%20rate%20mortgages [Accessed 23 November 2020].

Johnson, R.R., and Horan, S.M., 2013, 'Human capital and behavioural biases: Why investors don't diversify enough,' *The Journal of Wealth Management*, 16, 1, pp. 9–21.

Khanna, M., 2019, 'Bereaved Are Burdened with Record High Funeral Debt', *Royal London*, 4 September 2019. Available at www.royallondon.com/media/press-releases/2019/september/bereaved-are-burdened-with-record-high-funeral-debt/ [Accessed 23 November 2020].

Legal and General, *Deadline to Breadline: Myths and Misconceptions* [online]. Available at https://prod-epi.legalandgeneral.com/landg-assets/adviser/files/protection/sales-aid/deadline-to-breadline-report-2020.pdf [Accessed 21 March 2021].

Lynch, J.T., 2009, 'The Unspoken Need for Life Insurance', *Journal of Financial Service Professionals*, March, pp. 32–33.

Mahdzan, N.S., and Diacon, S., 2008, *Protection Insurance and Financial Wellbeing*. Available at www.researchgate.net/publication/275209568_Protection_Insurance_and_Financial_Wellbeing [Accessed 23 November 2020].

Madura, J., 2014, *Personal Finance* (Pearson: London and New York).

The Money Charity, 2020, *The Money Statistics*, November 2020 [online]. Available at https://themoneycharity.org.uk/media/November-2020-Money-Statistics.pdf [Accessed 21 March 2021].

Nettleton, S., and Burrows, R., 1998, 'Mortgage Debt, Insecure Home Ownership and Health: An Exploratory Analysis', *Sociology of Health & Illness*, 20 (5), p. 735. Available at https://doi.org/10.1111/1467-9566.00127 [Accessed 30 April 2021].

NGI Residential Mortgages, *Rise and Fall: Historical Interest Rates in UK, 1979–2019*. Available at www.ngiresidential.co.uk/rise-and-fall-historical-interest-rates-in-the-uk-1979-2019/ [Accessed 23 November 2020].

Osborne, H., 2021, 'UK homebuyers offered first 40-year fixed-rate mortgage', *The Guardian* [online]. Available at https://www.theguardian.com/money/2021/mar/10/uk-40-year-fixed-rate-mortgage-habito-deposit-loan. [Accessed 30 April 2021].

Royal London, 2017, *Reality Bites: The Cost of Critical Illness* [online]. Available at https://adviser.royallondon.com/globalassets/docs/protection/brp8pd0004-critical-illness-report.pdf [Accessed 30 April 2021].

Royal London, 2019, *Bereaved Are Burdened With Record High Funeral Debt*, 4 September 2019 [online]. Available at www.royallondon.com/media/press-releases/2019/september/bereaved-are-burdened-with-record-high-funeral-debt/ [Accessed 30 April 2021].

Smith, J., 2020, *Critical Illness Cover* (Royal London) [online]. Available at https://studio.royallondon.com/docs/reportcic-example.pdf [Accessed 30 April 2021].

SunLife, 2020, *Funeral Costs in the UK* [online]. Available at www.sunlife.co.uk/funeral-costs/#:~:text=In%202020%2C%20the%20average%20basic,65%25%20in%20the%20last%20decade [Accessed 23 November 2020].

Which, 2021, *What Is Mortgage Payment Protection Insurance?*. Available at https://www.which.co.uk/money/mortgages-and-property/mortgages/what-is-mortgage-protection-insurance-a912h5h1z67y. [Accessed 30 April 2021].

Chapter Eleven
Planning your purchase

Home ownership may be right for some, but not for others. Some people do not want to be tied to a mortgage and carry big financial commitments. They enjoy the freedom of renting and do not want the stresses and financial worries that homeownership can bring.

However, homeownership can bestow financial rewards and personal satisfaction in three ways:

1 **Higher disposable income**. Many people spend less on mortgage payments than on rents because interest rates have been low since the financial crisis of 2008.

In 2018–19, for example, homeowners in the UK spent on average 18 per cent of their household income on mortgage payments, whereas social renters spent 27 per cent of their household income on rent, and private renters 33 per cent (English Housing Survey, 2018–19, p. 18). Homeowners, therefore, have more disposable income, giving them a greater scope to save or spend their extra cash on other things.

Besides paying much less on mortgage payments, owning a home forces you to spend less now and save for the future because mortgage payments are a form of contractual saving where you have to make regular payments. This enables you to build wealth to fund your future needs.

2   **Enjoyment**. Home ownership is a big decision that can bring you enjoyment that is rooted in feelings of security, stability, peace of mind, freedom and control. If you have a house that you can afford, you'll enjoy making it into the home of your dreams. You'll be able to establish roots in your area because no one can ask you to leave. You will have peace of mind and many options.

3   **Wealth**. When you rent, your money is gone forever. But when you pay your mortgage, you build up equity in your property. This represents the amount of property wealth you have.

Wealth in your home can give you the power to do things in life. For some people, equity in their home can act as a line of credit because you can borrow more money from a bank against your property and use the fund to carry out home improvements, set up a business or buy additional properties to create residual income.

Property wealth can also give you peace of mind. When you own your home, especially when it is paid off, you have a big safety net in the event of job loss or other emergency because you know that you will always have a roof over your head.

If you have a big house, you can downsize and release some money to do other things you enjoy, without having to worry about making money.

Risks

Buying a house requires you to take on big risks. There is a risk that the value of the house might fall and that you might experience the pain of negative equity as you try to sell.

There is also a risk that you cannot pay your mortgage payments and suffer the distress of repossession. These latent fears make some people reluctant to buy, but the good news is that these risks can be managed.

The keys to successful home ownership lie in choosing the right property and being able to pay monthly mortgage payments over the agreed term. Choosing the property carefully and planning for the long term can help you reduce these risks.

Right type of property

Careful choice of property ensures that its value can always be maintained, whatever the market conditions, and avoids negative equity.

In order to find a right kind of property, it is essential to undertake a lot of research into the characteristics that make a property desirable as this affects prices of a property and the ease of re-selling.

We have already discussed the factors that make a property desirable in Chapter 4. In summary, there are 7 criteria to help you choose a good property:

1 **Safety**: safe area with low crime
2 **Space**: spacious property and neighbourhood (a lot of green space)
3 **Schools**: close to good schools
4 **Supermarkets**: proximity to supermarkets
5 **Stations**: close to stations (railway station or Tube station)
6 **Sports and stadiums**: near a sports venue or football stadium
7 **Special**: close to a good hospital, university, pub or water

If a property can meet as many of these 7 criteria as possible, it will be more desirable and reduce the chance of negative equity whatever the market conditions.

Ability to pay monthly mortgage payments

Besides negative equity, the other worry is repossession, as a result of the inability to pay the mortgage. The key reason why many people cannot pay their mortgage is due to a loss of income.

There are three ways to reduce this risk and can be summarised as the PIE principle.

a. **Planning for the future**: Ensuring that you can always pay your mortgage on time involves planning ahead and adopting financial discipline. You need to live within your means and do not spend more than you earn. This allows you to avoid debt, save money, build a financial buffer and achieve financial resilience.
b. **Income protection policy**: Long-term illness can drain any amount of money you may have and therefore an income protection policy is highly recommended as this will provide a replacement income in the event of ill health. Taking out an insurance policy enables you to transfer your personal risks to an insurance company and give you peace of mind.
c. **Emergency fund**: Having an emergency fund is critical because it enables you to deal with any emergencies, such as a boiler or car break-down, leaks or repairs. Financial advisers generally recommend holding enough money sufficient to cover at least 3–6 months of expenses.

George Clason, in *The Richest Man in Babylon*, offers five wise principles to help you manage money:

1 **Start saving**: Savings are necessary because they provide a pot of money which can be used as an emergency fund (recommend putting aside 10 per cent of income).
2 **Control expenditure**: A golden rule is that expenditure must be less than income to avoid debt and have surplus income for investment.
3 **Make your home a profitable investment**: For many people their home is an important source of wealth and so it is important to make a wise decision.
4 **Insure a future income**: Ill health can have a devastating impact and so it is important to insure a future income stream.
5 **Increase your ability to earn**: Prices tend to rise over time, and so it is important to ensure that earnings are higher than prices. Continuous learning or professional development can help increase individual earnings over time.

By adopting these principles, you can avoid financial difficulties and stress that come from money worries. You will make better use of money available and enjoy a feeling of financial security that wise money management can bring.

Moreover, you will have the confidence that you can always meet your financial and mortgage commitments. This in turn gives you peace of mind and confers much enjoyment that home ownership can bestow.

Reference

English Housing Survey Headline Report, 2018–19 [online]. Available at https://assets.publishing.service.gov.uk/government/uploads/system/uploads/attachment_data/file/860076/2018-19_EHS_Headline_Report.pdf [Accessed 14 November 2020].

Index

Note: Page numbers in *italics* indicate a figure and page numbers in **bold** indicate a table on the corresponding page.

Printed in the United States
by Baker & Taylor Publisher Services